CW01665150

An Introduction to Bookkeeping

Suitable for the

AAT Accounting Qualification in

Processing Bookkeeping Transactions
Control Accounts, Journals and the Banking System
and AAT Certificate in Bookkeeping

Study Manual

(4th EDITION)

Alan Dawson, B.Ed (Hons), MAAT

Edited by Rose Crockett BA (Hons)

PremierBooks

PremierBooks

Premier Books is the trading name for RSH Associates Ltd. Copyright © Alan Dawson August 2013. All rights reserved. No part of this publication may be reproduced, stored in a retrieval system, or transmitted in any form by any means, electronic, mechanical, photocopying, recording or otherwise, without prior written permission of the publisher.

Whilst every care has been taken in the accuracy of the compilation of this text it is for training purposes only. No responsibility for loss occasioned to any person acting or refraining from acting as a result of any material in this publication can be accepted by the publishers.

Published by:

Premier Books Ltd
Prince Henry Drive
Queens Road
Immingham
North East Lincolnshire
DN40 1QY
Telephone 01469 515444

Contents

	Introduction	vi
Chapter 1	**Accounting roles and transactions**	1
Chapter 2	**Selling goods and services**	11
Chapter 3	**VAT and legal considerations**	33
Chapter 4	**Recording sales and sales returns**	47
Chapter 5	**Cash receipts and cash sales**	75
Chapter 6	**Dealing with banks**	101
Chapter 7	**Recording purchases**	113
Chapter 8	**Making payments**	131
Chapter 9	**Petty Cash**	155
Chapter 10	**Wages and Salaries**	169
Chapter 11	**Methods of communication**	183
Chapter 12	**Less common transactions**	195
Chapter 13	**The cash book and bank statement**	211
Chapter 14	**Journals and the Trial Balance**	223
	Answers to Practice Questions	247

The Author

Alan Dawson

Certificate of Education

Bachelor of Education (Hons)

Member of the Association of Accounting Technicians

Qualified Teacher and Assessor

Alan is a qualified teacher. He gained his honours degree in education from Nottingham University and he went on to teach Mathematics, Modern Languages and Music in schools for 18 years.

He then turned his attention to accountancy, qualifying from the AAT and taking up various accounting roles both in private practice and industry. He spent 6 years in a large company in management accounts while at the same time taking private clients for help with bookkeeping, payroll, VAT and taxation.

From March 2006 he has been a tutor at Premier Training, with over 300 students worldwide under his guidance at one time or another.

Introduction

This study manual will provide you with all the knowledge and skill to succeed in the AAT Processing Bookkeeping Transactions and Control Accounts, Journals and the Banking Systems examinations and the AAT Certificate in Bookkeeping assessments. It is suitable both for home study courses and also classroom based students. All the answers to the questions have been included at the back of the book. In addition to the Study Manual, the publishers have produced a Revision Kit containing additional questions and activities for you to further practice your bookkeeping skills. The answers to the questions in the Revision Kit are given at the end of the book.

The reasons why people take up an accountancy course are varied, but if you are interested in figures and dealing with money then you will certainly enjoy the course.

Accounting is as old as civilisation. Man always has a need to record who owns what and to record trading activities, and much of what we know about the day to day activities of ancient people comes from accounting records.

From about 4000 BC in Sumaria small clay balls were used to keep track of a person's wealth. Different sizes and different shapes were used to represent the various items such as sheep or grain.

Since it was more convenient to trade in these tokens (it's far easier to transfer a clay ball than 100 sheep) it eventually developed into what we now call money. The first coins were developed around the 7th Century BC and the Ancient Greeks used silver drachmas from 5th Century BC. Coinage had a legal standard now and along with that came the need to account for what coinage each person had.

The Romans are known for their building of roads, buildings and aqueducts, but Rome also had a complex finance system which included tax collections, contracts and corporations. Obviously there was even more need to keep track of transactions by a more sophisticated method of keeping records. Accountants were even more in demand.

With the Crusades, beginning about 1000 AD, a demand for exotic Eastern goods developed which demanded more complex trading relationships. A knowledge of costs and potential revenues was now needed. The businesses became larger where the owner could not do everything himself and so there was a need for better recording of transactions, and a business's wealth.

Modern bookkeeping is based on double entry (you'll find out what this is later in this book). The first evidence of double entry bookkeeping comes from Italy around 1200 but the first book to contain a detailed description was 'Summa de Arithmetica, Geometrica, Proportioni et Proportionalite' (1494) by Luca Pacioli (1447-1517), a Franciscan monk and mathematician. (But don't worry; you don't have to be a mathematician to do accounts).

Wealth, trade and the development of technology are the reason we have a civilized world, but the need to account for it is of equal importance. The Italian merchants became successful and powerful partly through their superior financial knowledge.

Understanding costs and revenues, they were better equipped than their competitors to make sound financial judgements. From this prosperity came the start of the modern world as we know it.

Chapter 1

Accounting Roles and Transactions

In this chapter we will be looking at the differing roles within an accounting system as well as the different organisations themselves. We will also look at the different transactions which may take place and the ways businesses set up their accounting systems.

Before we look at the mechanics of recording transactions we need to have a basic understanding of the different roles within an accounting system as well as the different types of business.

Bookkeeper

A bookkeeper is someone who records all the financial transactions of a business. Each type of transaction is stored in a different file called a book, hence the name bookkeeper. The most important actions of any business is buying and selling. The bookkeeper will record the details of all day to day sales and purchases in **day books**. They are called day books because daily transactions are recorded here. There will be a day book for sales and another for purchases. Obviously sales and purchases will involve the transfer of money, so the bookkeeper will also record the movement in and out of the business in a **cash book**. All books which record these transactions as they happen are called **books of prime entry**. In this case 'prime' means 'first' so these books are where the transactions are first recorded.

The bookkeeper is unlikely to be present at every transaction, so he or she will record transactions in the books of prime entry from **prime documents**. Typically a prime document is a receipt or an invoice, although we shall see later that other documents may fall into this category.

Accountant

An accountant is someone who deals with the presentation and interpretation of the figures. You will see later that there are rules and regulations covering the presentation of financial information. Financial information may include a **profit & loss statement** (also known as an **income statement** or a **statement of revenue and expense**). A profit & loss statement (or P&L) shows a business's financial performance.

Financial information may also be shown in a **balance sheet**. A balance sheet shows a business's assets, liabilities and net worth at a specific point in time.

The accountant may be responsible for advising on, and calculating taxation. Individuals and companies are all liable to taxation. Unlike employees, people with businesses are responsible for their own tax issues and the payment of amounts due. Accountants may calculate how much tax is due and complete the forms which are to be presented to **Her Majesty's Revenue and Customs** (HMRC). HMRC is the government department which deals with taxation in the UK.

An accountant may also be responsible for interpreting financial information. He or she may have to make decisions on future events in the business based on the business's past record. This may involve giving advice on the selling prices of goods, if it would be financially viable to go ahead with a new product, or whether to buy new machinery for the factory.

Accounting Technician

An Accounting Technician is someone who performs some of the duties of both the bookkeeper and the accountant. He or she may assist with the preparation of financial statements, deal with bookkeeping, look after and control budgets, monitor expenses and write reports. In many larger organisations, accounting technicians work alongside members of chartered accountancy bodies. In smaller organisations, they may be the only financially trained member of staff.

In practice the roles of the bookkeeper, accountant and accounting technician are all not as clearly defined as above, but this is a guide to the traditional duties of each.

Types of Business

There are three main types of business which will be dealt with in the AAT course.

Sole Trader

This is the business most dealt with in this Unit. The business will be owned and run by an individual. He or she will probably be responsible for most of the running of the business. He or she will be in charge of buying and selling goods or services and be in charge of hiring and firing staff. Many sole traders maintain their own books and then employ an accountant to prepare the final accounts ready for the tax calculation at the end of each financial year.

It is important to remember that a sole trader not only has the rights to all the profits a business makes, but also he or she is personally responsible for any losses. If a sole trader finds that he or she cannot pay his or her creditors from the business's income, then the money has to be found from the sole trader's personal belongings. For example, if a sole trader cannot keep up the repayments on the loan secured from the bank, the bank has the right to any or all of the sole trader's personal belongings until the debt has been repaid or the sole trader has no more belongings.

CHAPTER 1
Accounting Roles and Transactions

Partnerships

This is where a group of individuals come together to form a business. Typically there will be two to twenty individuals in a partnership and an agreement will have been made as to the proportion of profits to which each partner will be entitled. Partnerships are formed usually because, with more people involved in the business, there will be more expertise and money available to invest the company.

However, as with sole traders, the partners are personally responsible for any losses. In England and Wales they are 'jointly' responsible. All partners are equally responsible for all the debts of the business. They can only be sued as a group and not as an individual. In Scotland the law is slightly different. Here they are 'jointly and severally' liable, which means that in certain cases an individual partner can be sued, but if this partner doesn't have the resources to cover the suit then the other partners become liable for any amounts due.

Limited Company

A limited company is where a business is formed which is quite separate in legal terms from its 'owners'. The owners are **shareholders** but the company's finances are separate from the shareholders' personal finances. The shareholders have 'limited liability', meaning that they are only responsible for the amount of money they have invested (or guaranteed) to the company.

There are two main types of limited company. A **private limited company** may have one or more shareholders. The shares cannot be offered to the public. A **public limited company** (plc) must have at least two shareholders and must have issued shares worth at least £50,000. Both kinds of limited company must be registered at **Companies House** and each must appoint a director (at least two if it's a plc) who will manage the business. Each year a limited company must file its accounts with Companies House where the figures are open to the public. Profits are distributed to the shareholders each year (called **dividends**) in proportion to the number of shares owned. Some of the profit may be retained by the company for use within the company to pay future debts or for future investments.

Other Business Types

There are other types of businesses. So far we have only looked at the '**private sector**'. There are also '**public sector**' businesses which are owned or controlled by the Government. The public sector covers a wide range of organisations with different functions e.g.

Central government
Local government
Health trusts
Educational bodies e.g. schools and colleges
Some corporations such as the BBC.

Then there is the '**voluntary sector**'. This includes charities or clubs. Typically they will have been established with the objective of addressing a social need, rather than simply to provide a service or generate revenue. Often they are non-profit making, or will reinvest revenue for the purpose of serving their client group or achieving their objective.

Organisational Structures

It may be becoming clear that the organisational structure of a business is dependent on the type of business. A small sole trader may do all the bookkeeping him- or herself. This is perfectly possible (although a lot of hard work) since the amount of information required will be limited. Basically all that is required in a one-man business is a list of what was sold and a list of what was bought. Taking the books to an accountant each year will be sufficient for the sole trader to see how well (or otherwise) the business is going and to satisfy HMRC regarding taxation.

In partnerships a little more work is required, although each partner will be responsible for his or her own tax liabilities. Since the company has more than one owner, a track of sales and purchases needs to be kept and the revenue and expenses created by each partner. It would be wise for a partnership to employ at least a bookkeeper to record the day to day transactions.

Limited companies will require more detailed accounting records. The format of the accounting records is regulated and more than simply what was bought and sold will need to be recorded and reported. Larger companies will have different departments for sales, purchases, wages, and **management accounts**. Management accountants assist management in decision-making, planning, and control. **Financial accountants** report the financial position and performance of a business.

Where there is more than one person in a company some sort of organisational structure will be required. The most common structure for larger businesses is the **hierarchical structure**. Responsibility passes from the director, to senior management, to middle management, and then to supervisors.

Then there is the '**tall**' structure. This has many levels of management with a long chain of responsibility.

Another structure is the '**flat**' structure.

The following pages show each structure in diagrammatic form.

Hierarchical Structure

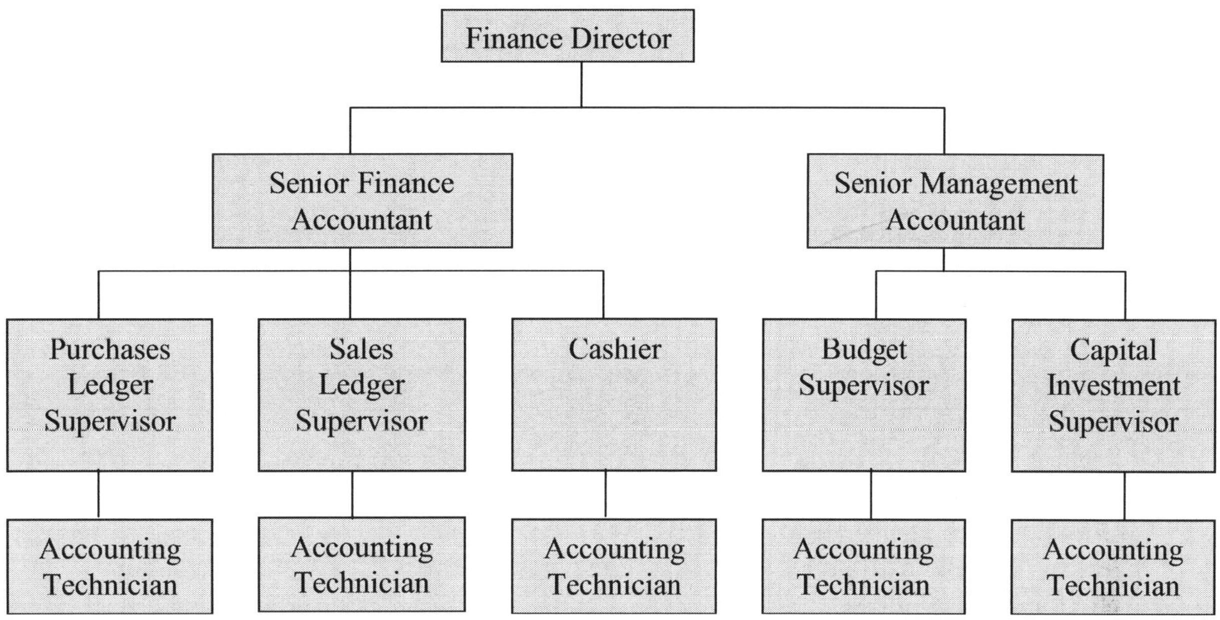

Tall Structure

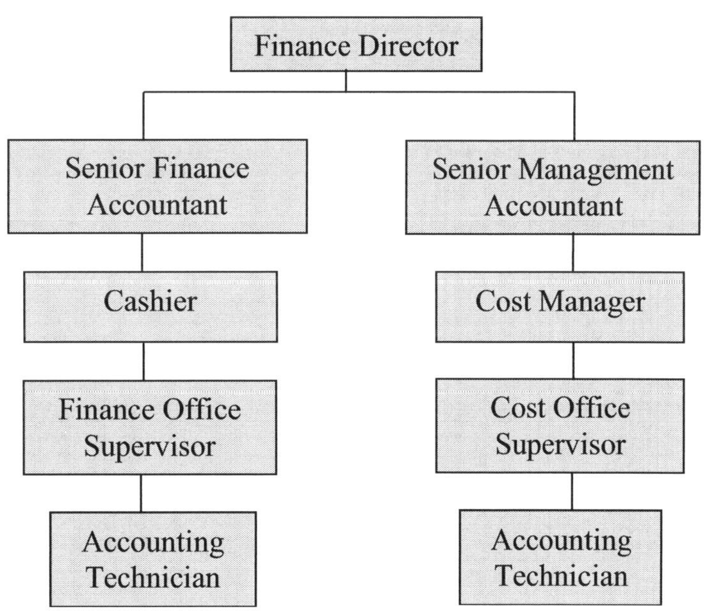

Flat Structure

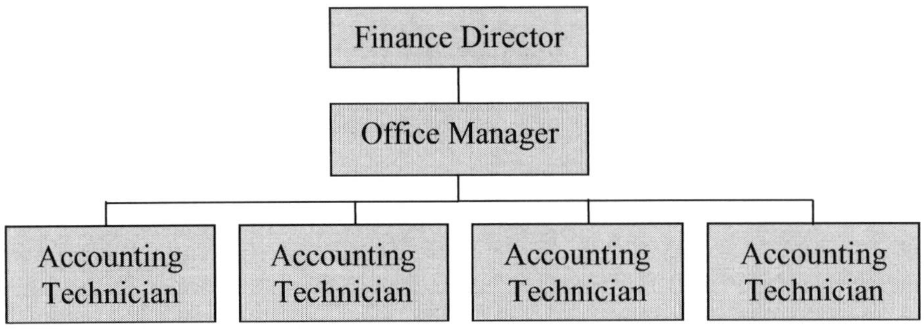

Each of the above structures has been shown in a **functional format**, with each position showing what its function is. They could have been shown by **regional area** (Finance Director North and Finance Director South for example), by **product** (Finance Director Private Vehicles and Finance Director Commercial Vehicles), or a structure could be set up for individual projects.

Accounting transactions

No matter what the business or how it is structured all businesses carry out transactions which are common to all.

All businesses sell goods or services
All businesses purchase goods and services and pay expenses
All businesses pay money into a bank account and make payments from it
All businesses pay wages or a remuneration of some kind.

All these transactions must be recorded in some form. Some small businesses simply collect all **invoices** and **receipts** and give them to the accountant at the end of the year so that the accountant can produce financial statements from them. An invoice is a list of goods or services sold and given to the purchaser for payment. A receipt is a written acknowledgement that payment has been made for goods or services. Some small businesses record these transactions in their books as they occur, making the accountant's work easier and less time consuming (and therefore usually less expensive). A larger business will need to employ staff to look after the recording of these transactions since it will not be physically possible to do this on one's own. Books can be kept either by hand (manually) or on a computer.

Retaining documents

Legally there are differing instructions on how long accounting documents are to be kept. The **Companies Act 2006** states that a public limited company must keep records for six years from the date they are drawn up. Since the accounting records are made up for the year, some documentation from the beginning of the year will need to be kept, which in effect will make it seven years.

The **Companies Act 2006** states that private limited companies must keep similar records for three years.

The **Finance Act 1997** amended the requirement in the **Value Added Tax Act 1994** so that accounting records for VAT should be kept for six years.

The Income Tax (Pay As You Earn) Regulations 2003 states that employers must keep payroll records for not less than three years.

The **Limitations Act 1980** requires that any action for a contract or fraud expires after six years. However, documents may be required for longer if such action is taken within the six years.

The **Taxes Management Act 1970** says that an assessment for tax can be made up to six years after the end of the period to which it relates, but personal tax documents need only be kept for 1 year and 10 months.

The **Data Protection Act** states that personal data processed for any purpose or purposes shall not be kept for longer than is necessary for that purpose or those purposes.

Other legislation requires certain documents to be retained for between 1 year and permanently.

So you can see that the legislation is confusing. If documents were never destroyed the business would accumulate a large amount of paperwork taking up space which could best be used for other purposes. It is therefore essential that the business has a policy on document retention. For most accounting documents this is often 6 years after the end of the period to which it relates. In most cases this will be sufficient to cover all possible claims made by employees, HMRC or customers. If documents are not available when they should be a fine will be imposed.

Once the retention period has elapsed the paperwork should not be simply thrown away in the general waste. It contains confidential information even though the information is old. The documents should be shredded or disposed of in a similar way so that private information does not find its way into the public domain.

In the next chapters we will look at some of the documents associated with financial transactions.

Chapter Summary

A bookkeeper records the financial transactions of a business in day books, while an accountant presents and interprets this data.

A bookkeeper records transactions in day books and a cash book (which are books of prime entry) from prime documents.

The data from the books of prime entry is used to produce financial statements such as a profit and loss statement and a balance sheet.

There are three main types of business organisation: sole traders, partnerships and limited companies.

Businesses have structures according to size and type. The three main structures are hierarchical, tall and flat. The structure may be organised according to function, region or product.

All businesses have to record similar transactions. Businesses will record sales, purchases and bank transactions.

It is a legal requirement that documents are retained for specific periods of time. All businesses should have a policy on document retention.

CHAPTER 1
Accounting Roles and Transactions

Practice Questions

Chapter 1

1.1

a) What type of business is run and owned by an individual?

b) What type of business is owned by its shareholders?

c) What type of business is run and owned by a group of associated people?

d) If you bought shares from a stockbroker who traded in shares on the stock market, what kind of business would you be investing in?

1.2

a) Traditionally, who records day to day transactions in books of prime entry?

   a) Bookkeeper
   b) Accountant
   c) Accounting Technician

b) Traditionally, who prepares a Profit & Loss account and a Balance Sheet?

   a) Bookkeeper
   b) Accountant
   c) Accounting Technician

CHAPTER 1
Accounting Roles and Transactions

1.3

a) As an Accounting Technician, you work in an organisation with a long chain of command. There are many levels of management and supervision. Is this likely to be:

a) A Hierarchical structure
b) A Tall structure
c) A Flat Structure?

b) As an Accounting Technician, you work in an organisation with few layers of management. You are responsible to the office manager, who oversees all of your colleagues as well. The office manager is responsible directly to the Managing Director. Is this likely to be:

a) A Hierarchical structure
b) A Tall structure
c) A Flat Structure?

c) As an Accounting Technician, you work in an organisation where you are responsible to a manager for your area of work. Other managers are responsible for colleagues who work in other areas of accounts. There are various levels within the organisation and at each stage one person has a number of workers directly under them according to their area of work. Is this likely to be:

a) A Hierarchical structure
b) A Tall structure
c) A Flat Structure?

Chapter 2

Selling Goods and Services

In this chapter we will be looking at the process of selling goods or services. We will look at some of the documents used when making a sale.

We will look at the calculation of invoice totals along with any discounts offered.

We will see how VAT is calculated when dealing with customers.

The primary function of any commercial business is to sell goods or services with the intention of making a profit.

Documents involved in making a sale

Before you can sell anything, your customers will need to know how much you are selling the goods or services for. You will need a price list, a catalogue or you may advertise the price on the actual goods. Some businesses cannot give a standard price, as goods and services will vary from sale to sale. Typical examples are builders and decorators. In these cases the seller will provide an **estimate** or a **quote**.

In legal terms there is a lot of difference between an estimate and a quote. An estimate is a rough idea based on guess-work as to how much the job will cost the customer. However, the amount stated is not binding and the price may change according to different circumstances which the supplier may come across. A quote, on the other hand cannot be changed once it has been accepted by the customer. It is possible, though, to state exactly what the quote is for and that additional charges may be incurred if certain unexpected circumstances occur.

An example of a quotation is shown on the next page.

DAWSON SUPPLIES
43 Scartho Rd, Immingham, DN20 6NP
Tel. 01469 515444

R Patel
132 Anglian Way
Norwich
NR3 6FG

Date: 18/08/2014

Thank you for your enquiry regarding our rolls of blue cotton dress material.
I can quote as follows:

50 Rolls of blue cotton dress material @ £75.00 per roll, excluding VAT.
There will be a delivery charge of £25.00

This quote is valid for 3 months

Our terms are strictly Cash on Delivery

A D Dawson

Director

It is good practice to include the period for which the quotation is valid and to state the terms of payment and any delivery charges. You will also often see 'E&OE'. This stands for 'Errors and Omissions Excepted'. It means that if a genuine error has been made in the preparation of the quote, then the supplier cannot be held to it. Of course the quotation should be signed and dated.

So let us suppose the customer is happy with the quote and decides he or she wants the goods. A small business would probably just phone up and say he or she wants the goods. Larger companies will supply a **purchase order**.

A purchase order has:

- an individual reference number
- a product code if available (an example of coding which is particularly useful when using a computer accounts package)
- a quantity
- a description of the goods in full
- a unit price and a total price (not really necessary as the supplier will know the price, but it is useful as a check that the correct price has been quoted)
- an authorising signature and date (most important as the supplier will probably not fulfil the order without this).
- an invoice address and delivery address

R Patel
132 Anglian Way, Norwich, NR3 6FG
PURCHASE ORDER

Dawson Supplies
43 Scartho Road
Immingham
DN20 6NP

Invoice Address: 132 Anglian Way, Norwich, NR3 6FG

Delivery Address: 27 High Street, Norwich, NR1 3ZT

Purchase Order No: 5379

Order Date: 21st August 2014

Part Code	Qty	Description	Unit Price	Total Price
	50	Rolls Blue Cotton Dress Material	£75.00	£3,750.00
			Purchase Order Total:	**£3,750.00**

Authorised : *R Patel* Date *21/08/2014*

All orders are raised subject to our Terms and Conditions of trade. A full copy is available on request. E&OE. All prices exclude VAT.

A purchase order is a legal document. Once the purchase order has been accepted by the seller then a contract exists between the buyer and seller. The seller is deemed to have accepted the purchase order 48 hours after issue.

We will see more about the legal side of buying and selling later in this book.

If the delivery is not immediate (maybe the supplier has to wait for their own delivery, or it may be that the buyer doesn't want the goods immediately) an **advice note** may be issued. This confirms that the purchase has been accepted and it also lets the customer know when the goods will be delivered or that the goods are on their way.

So let us now suppose that the goods are ready for delivery. The supplier will send a **delivery note** with the goods. When the goods reach their destination the buyer will check the delivery to ensure that the correct goods and quantity of goods have been delivered. If the receiver is happy then he or she will sign the delivery note. There are usually at least two parts to the delivery note. One part will stay with the customer. It is usually passed on to the accounts department as a check that the goods have actually been delivered. The other part will be returned to the supplier as proof of delivery. The customer cannot then say they will not pay because the goods have not been delivered.

Dawson Supplies

43 Scartho Rd, Immingham, DN20 6NP

DELIVERY NOTE

NO. 23198

To :	R Patel	Your Order Number :	5379
Address :	27 High Street	Date Sent :	25th August 2014
	Norwich	Per Invoice Number :	13608
	NR1 3ZT	Our Contact Person :	J Grimston
Attention :	J Crockett	Telephone :	01469 515444

Quantity Delivered	Description
50	Rolls of Blue Cotton Dress Material

Goods received in good order					
Name :		Signature :		Date :	

A delivery note usually has an identifying number. Of course the description should match what has actually been delivered. No price is shown as this is not needed at the moment. This will be shown in the invoice (see next). However, a reference to the purchase order is usually made so the buyer can reference the delivery note to the purchase order.

An **invoice** is a document which itemises the goods delivered or services rendered, specifying the terms of the sale and the price.

CHAPTER 2
Selling Goods and Services

The invoice is a legal document and if it is to record VAT (**Value Added Tax**), must have certain items included. Details of what must be included on a VAT invoice are dealt with in the Indirect Tax Unit of the AAT level 3 Diploma. For now you should know that VAT is a tax on purchases. You must register with HMRC for VAT when the value of all your sales reaches £79,000. (This figure is correct at the time of going to press, but readers should be aware that this figure changes regularly, usually annually. If you want to know the current registration threshold you should visit http://www.hmrc.gov.uk/vat/start/register/when-to-register.htm). When a company is registered, it must charge VAT on all its sales (apart from those items at zero rate and exempt). Again we will look at these in more detail in the Indirect Tax Unit of the AAT level 3 Diploma. The current rate of VAT is 20% on most items.

An invoice will include:

The name and address of the supplier.

The address to which the invoice must be sent.

The address where the goods are to be sent (if different from the invoice address)

The invoice has a unique number (essential if VAT is to be charged). The numbers are sequential so it is easy to trace and easy to see if one is missing.

The VAT registration number if the company is registered for VAT.

Customers may be allocated a reference number. This will help identify the customer particularly if there are a large number of customers. A customer reference number will be essential if using a computer accounting program.

The original purchase order number will be shown. This helps reference the invoice to the purchase order.

The date of the invoice. This is important as the terms will state how long the customer has to pay. The **tax point** has significance when VAT is paid to HMRC. It is usually the same date as the invoice was raised. We will look at when it is not in the Indirect Tax Unit at level 3.

There may be a product code (e.g. B1003). This is useful in identifying the product if there are a large number of products. It is also much simpler to refer to the product code if for example the product is 'a box of 100 x 3 inch nails' It is also essential for stock control if a computer is used.

There is a precise description of the goods and the quantity should be the same as the purchase order.

The price should be shown both per unit and for the total.

Discounts may be offered for regular customers or for purchasing goods in bulk. This is usually expressed as a percentage and is taken off the total before the VAT is calculated.

If an invoice mentions the **net** amount it means that this is the amount before VAT has been added. (The amount after VAT has been added is referred to as the **gross** amount.)

VAT is calculated on the net amount at the current rate and the rate appropriate to the goods sold.

A total for the invoice will be shown which included the goods (less any discount) plus the VAT charged.

DAWSON SUPPLIES

45 Scartho Street, Immingham, IM15 2BH

Invoice

Number: 13608

Invoice to

R Patel
132 Anglian Way
Norwich
NR3 6FG

Deliver to

R Patel
27 High Street
Norwich
NR1 3ZT

Date/ tax point: 25th August 2014

Account: RP01

Your reference: 5379

VAT Reg: GB 0369 4928 36

Product Code	Item	Quantity	Price £	Total £
	Rolls of Blue Cotton Dress Material	50	75.00	3,750.00
Goods Total				3,750.00
Trade Discount @ _________%				-
Subtotal				3,750.00
VAT @ 20%				750.00
Invoice Total				**4,500.00**

Terms
COD
Ex-works
E&OE

You should also note some of the **terms** you may find on an invoice:

> We have already looked at *E&OE* which means errors and omissions excepted.
> *30 days net* means that payment in full should be made within 30 days. (Other periods are possible such as 7 days or 60 days).
> *COD* stands for Cash on Delivery. Payment must be made when the goods are delivered.
> *Ex-works* means that the price of the goods does not include delivery whereas *carriage paid* means that the price **does** include delivery.
> *Settlement Discount* may be offered for early payment. This is usually a further percentage discount if the invoice is paid (for example) within 7 days. The rules for charging VAT are altered if a settlement discount is offered as we shall see later in this chapter. (Settlement discounts are also known as *cash discounts*).

Invoices books are generally in multiple parts. There will be a copy to send to the customer and a copy to keep for your own records. More copies can be kept if the invoice is required by more than one department.

Discounts

Discounts are offered as a way of increasing sales. There are different categories of discount.

Discounts to the general public are usually shown as a 'sale price'. The reason for offering a discount could be to encourage people to buy slow moving stock, or stock which is soon to become out-of-date or obsolete. Alternatively it may be to get us into the shop where we can be encouraged to buy other things at full price. The discounted item is then known as a 'loss leader' where little or no profit will be made on that item (or in some cases even a loss) in the hope that customers will buy other goods where the profit **will** be made.

Discounts may be offered for bulk buying. This is very common. I'm sure we have all seen offers like 'buy one get one free'. Everyone knows that if we buy one orange from the supermarket it will often cost more per orange than if we buy (say) a dozen. In business this **bulk discount** may be offered as a percentage. For example a supplier may offer a 10% discount if the customer buys more than 100 units or spends more than £500. Many things offered in bulk are offered at a discount because there are fewer costs involved, whether this be distribution cost, selling costs or just basic administration costs.

Another type of discount is the **trade discount**. Many DIY stores offer trade discounts to business customers 'in the trade'. This is a way of encouraging people who are likely to be repeat customers to buy from this store rather than going elsewhere. Offer your customer a good deal and he or she is likely to come again and again. Trade discounts are usually offered at a percentage of the total cost.

Calculating discounts

So how does this affect the invoice we raise? Well, let us take an example of an invoice where a 10% trade discount has been given.

Calculating a trade discount

Dawson Supplies is supplying R Patel with 50 rolls of cotton dress material at £75.00 per roll. R Patel is a dress maker and so Dawson Supplies offers R Patel a 10% trade discount.

Dawson Supplies will calculate the invoice as follows:

1 Calculate the total price before discount
50 x £75.00 = £3750.00

2 Calculate the trade discount
£3750.00 x 10%. (You can either use the percentage key on your calculator or multiply by 10 and divide by 100) = £375.00

3 Calculate the net price before VAT
£3750.00 - £375.00 = £3375.00

4 Calculate the VAT (at 20%). Again you can either use the percentage key or multiply by 20 and divide by 100)
£3375.00 x 20% (or 20/100) = £675.00
(Notice how the VAT is rounded down to the nearest whole penny)

5 Calculate the total invoice price
£3375.00 + £675.00 = £4050.00

You should note how the trade discount is taken off **before** calculating VAT, since the tax is only on the money transferred. (We shall look at VAT in more detail later in this chapter.)

Now let us take a look at how the invoice would look with the trade discount taken off.

DAWSON SUPPLIES

45 Scartho Street, Immingham, IM15 2BH

Invoice

Number: 13608

Invoice to

R Patel
132 Anglian Way
Norwich
NR3 6FG

Deliver to

R Patel
27 High Street
Norwich
NR1 3ZT

Date/ tax point:	25th August 2014
Account:	RP01
Your reference:	5379
VAT Reg:	GB 0369 4928 36

Product Code	Item	Quantity	Price £	Total £
	Rolls of Blue Cotton Dress Material	50	75.00	3,750.00
Goods Total				3,750.00
Trade Discount @ 10%				375.00
Subtotal				3,375.00
VAT @ 20%				675.00
Invoice Total				**4050.00**

Terms
30 days net
COD
Ex-works
E&OE

Settlement Discount (also known as Cash Discount)

Settlement discounts have been left until now because of the way they alter the calculation of an invoice.

A settlement discount may be offered for early payment of an invoice. It encourages the customer to pay sooner for the goods than the invoice allows. Under the 'terms' a typical entry would be '*2.5% settlement discount for payment within 7 days*'. This would mean that 2.5% would be taken off the **net** amount of the invoice if the customer settled the invoice within the 7 days.

IMPORTANT POINTS

1 VAT is charged on the amount **less** the settlement discount.

1. The invoice total is calculated as the reduced amount of VAT plus the net amount of the goods **before** the settlement discount is taken off.

2. Since the VAT has already been reduced, any settlement discount which is taken must be calculated on the **net** amount.

It is important that you distinguish between each type of discount, not only for the preparation of the invoice, but also the way each type is recorded in the accounting books. We shall see later in this book how discounts are recorded in the accounts books.

Let us go through the calculation of an invoice with both a trade and settlement discount. Take care that the figures you arrive at are reasonable. Many students have calculated discounts of more than the goods simply because they pushed the wrong button on their calculator and did not look to see if it was a reasonable figure.

We will follow the same example as above with the 10% trade discount, but this time we will offer a 3% settlement discount for payment within 7 days.

Calculating a trade discount and a settlement discount

Dawson Supplies is supplying R Patel with 50 rolls of cotton dress material at £75.00 per roll. R Patel is a dress maker and so Dawson Supplies offers R Patel a 10% trade discount. R Patel has credit facilities with Dawson Supplies and is allowed 30 days to settle the invoice, but in order to increase cash flow, Dawson Supplies offers R Patel a 3% settlement discount if the invoice is paid within 7 days.

Dawson Supplies will calculate the invoice as follows:

1. Calculate the total price before trade discount
   50 x £75.00 = £3750.00

2. Calculate the trade discount (as before)
   £3750.00 x 10% (or 10/100) = £375.00

3. Calculate the net price (as before)
   £3750.00 - £375.00 = £3375.00

4. Calculate the Settlement Discount on the net amount
   £3375.00 x 3% (or 3/100) = £101.25

5. Calculate the reduced amount. (You must simply keep a note of this as it is not shown on the invoice)
   £3375.00 - £101.25 = £3273.75

6. Calculate the VAT on the reduced amount
   £3273.75 x 20% (or 20/100) = £654.75
   (Notice how we have rounded the VAT down to the nearest penny again)

7. Calculate the total of the invoice
   £3375.00 + £654.75 = £4029.75

8. (Optional) Some companies will state the amount of discount if the settlement discount is taken. This will be the same calculation as in step 4 above.
   £3375.00 x 3% (or 3/100) = £101.25

Now let's look at the invoice which would be raised when the trade **and** settlement discounts are applied.

DAWSON SUPPLIES

45 Scartho Street, Immingham, IM15 2BH

Invoice

Number: 13608

Invoice to

R Patel
132 Anglian Way
Norwich
NR3 6FG

Deliver to

R Patel
27 High Street
Norwich
NR1 3ZT

Date/ tax point: 25th August 2014

Account: RP01

Your reference: 5379

VAT Reg: GB 0369 4928 36

Product Code	Item	Quantity	Price £	Total £
	Rolls of Blue Cotton Dress Material	50	75.00	3,750.00
Goods Total				3,750.00
Trade Discount @ 10%				375.00
Subtotal				3,375.00
VAT @ 20%				654.75
Invoice Total				**4029.75**

Terms
3% settlement discount for settlement within 7 days, other wise 30 days net — £101.25
Ex-works
E&OE

If the customer pays within the 7 days then he or she will only pay £4029.75 - £101.25 = £3928.50, but if the customer pays after the 7 days then £4029.75 will be due.

EXAM ALERT!

The calculation of invoices with trade and settlement discounts is a favourite exam topic. Make sure you understand it and revise this section again if you're not completely sure before you continue with the book.

Other documents relating to sales

Let us suppose that R Patel receives his dress material but two of the rolls have a flaw in them. Mr Patel will not want to pay for the faulty goods so he will inform Dawson Supplies that he no longer wants these rolls as they are faulty. In Dawson Supplies' books it will still be showing that R Patel owes £3375.00. (Remember that the goods have not yet been paid for). The rolls will probably be sent back with a **returns note.**

R PATEL

132 Anglian Way, Norwich, NR3 6FG

RETURNS NOTE

To

Dawson Supplies
45 Scartho Street
Immingham
IM15 2BH

Description of item(s)	Quantity
Rolls of Blue Cotton Dress Material	*2*

REASON FOR RETURN: *Faulty Goods*

Signature

Date:

When the goods have been received back, Dawson Supplies will raise a **credit note**. A credit note is a refund document stating that the customer no longer owes part or all of the amount on an invoice. Why not just tear up the invoice? Well there are two main reasons.

First of all the credit note is proof that the original invoice does not need paying in full. Dawson Supplies may have forgotten that the invoice had been reduced in their books and they may try to pursue payment. The credit note is proof that Dawson Supplies had agreed the reduction.

Secondly, both companies will have recorded the invoice in their books. Unlike cash sales, credit sales are not paid for there and then so a cash refund is not an option. Simply crossing out an entry is also not an option. It is frowned upon to erase entries in books as this can often lead to fraud and misleading figures. A credit note is proof that the credit has been approved and taken place and it is also a record that the original sale was made but there was something wrong with it.

Let us have a look at the calculations for the credit note for the return of these two rolls.

The calculation takes exactly the same format as the original invoice. It is common sense to still take off the trade discount as it is the reduced amount which was charged and it should be the same reduced amount which is given back. However, to still offer a settlement discount when you are in effect giving money back may at first seem bizarre.

The reason is that the original invoice calculated the VAT on the reduced amount. If you don't subsequently take the settlement into account when calculating the Credit Note then you could finish up giving back more than you charged in the first place.

Take the invoice we prepared on p22. Let's suppose that R Patel wants to send it all back. If we ignore the settlement discount then the calculation on the credit note would be (£3375.00 + 20%) = (£3375.00 + 675.00) = £4050.00. You can see, though, that the original invoice was for £4029.75. If you didn't take the settlement discount into the calculations then you would be giving R Patel more back than you charged him.

EXAM ALERT!

The calculation of credit note figures is very likely to come up in your examination. The questions will either take the form of calculating the actual credit note or you may be given documents to check for their accuracy.

Let us see the calculation for the return of the two rolls.

Calculating a Credit Note

R Patel finds that two of the rolls of material are faulty. He is returning the rolls and has requested a credit note.

Dawson Supplies will calculate the Credit Note as follows:

1. Calculate the total price before trade discount
   2 x £75.00 = £150.00

2. Calculate the trade discount
   £150.00 x 10% (or 10/100) = £15.00

3. Calculate the net price
   £150.00 - £15.00 = £135.00

4. Calculate the Settlement Discount on the net amount
   £135.00 x 3% (or 3/100) = £4.05

5. Calculate the reduced amount. (You must simply keep a note of this as it is not shown on the credit note)
   £135.00 - £4.05 = £130.95

6. Calculate the VAT on the reduced amount
   £130.95 x 20% (or 20/100) = £26.19
   (Notice how we have rounded the VAT down to the nearest penny again)

7. Calculate the total of the credit note.
   £135.00 + £26.19 = £161.19

The credit note itself often looks very similar to the Invoice. Some companies try to make the distinction between an Invoice and a Credit Note more obvious by printing at least some of the credit note in red.

A credit note will include:

The number of the original invoice
The reason for the return
A unique number. Credit Notes have their own sequence of numbers

Otherwise the details are exactly like an invoice.

DAWSON SUPPLIES

45 Scartho Street, Immingham, IM15 2BH

Credit Note

Number: CN259

To

R Patel
132 Anglian Way
Norwich
NR3 6FG

Date/ tax point:	27th August 2014
Account:	RP01
Your reference:	5379
VAT Reg:	GB 0369 4928 36
Our invoice no.	13608

Product Code	Item	Quantity	Price £	Total £
	Rolls of Blue Cotton Dress Material	2	75.00	150.00
Goods Total				150.00
Trade Discount @ 10%				15.00
Subtotal				135.00
VAT @ 20%				26.19
Credit Total				**161.19**

Reason for Credit

2 Rolls Blue Cotton Dress Material faulty

The final document we will look at in this section is the **statement**.

Just as your bank statement will show the transactions which have occurred between you and your bank, so a statement of account for a customer will show all the transactions between the customer and the supplier.

As you have seen, a customer may have been allowed to pay their invoice after an agreed period of time (7 days, 30 days or even 60 days are typical). You can probably imagine that regular customers will have several outstanding invoices, so a statement of account is sent to the customer, usually monthly, so that both parties are aware what is still owed by the buyer to the supplier.

The statement will begin with the balance **b/f**. (Sometimes this is shown as b/d meaning brought down from the previous period). B/f stands for 'brought forward' and shows the amount still owing at the beginning of the month, or *brought forward* from the previous month.

Any new invoices will be added to the total and any payment will be taken from the total.

You must always remember to include any credit notes which have been issued, and (the one that so many students forget to include) any settlement discounts which have been taken. You must remember the settlement discount because if you don't the customer will still be showing as owing an amount, when in fact the account has been paid in full.

Let us take the example of the invoice from Dawson Supplies on p22 which includes the settlement discount.

The invoice will be shown on the statement as £4029.75. If the customer pays within the 7 days allowed he will pay just £3928.50(£4029.75 – £101.25). The statement will show the invoice amount of £4029.75 and the payment of £3928.50. Unless we include the settlement discount on the statement, R Patel will still be showing he owes £101.25.

The statement will finally show the remaining balance. This amount will be '**carried forward**' (c/f) to the next statement.

If you look at the statement of account on the next page you will notice that invoices (or any amounts which increase what is owed) are called debits and go on the left. Any amounts which decrease the amount owed are called credits and go on the right. We will look at debits and credits in much more detail later in this book, but for now remember which side each is on and what it means in the statement.

Transactions are listed in date order. You will note that only settlement discounts are included (not trade or bulk discounts since these are already given in the invoice figure). The settlement discounts are only stated once they have been taken and not when they are offered. After all, the customer may not pay within the time allowed to qualify for the discount.

STATEMENT OF ACCOUNT

DAWSON SUPPLIES

45 Scartho Street, Immingham, IM15 2BH

To

R Patel
132 Anglian Way
Norwich
NR3 6FG

Account RP01

Date 31st August 2014

Date	Details	Debit £	Credit £	Balance £
01/08/2014	Balance b/f	3671.52		3671.52
03/08/2014	Chq received		3561.38	110.14
03/08/2014	Disc allowed		110.14	0.00
07/08/2014	Inv 13295	3196.50		3196.50
14/08/2014	Inv 13458	2957.17		6153.67
21/08/2014	Inv 13598	3279.59		9433.26
25/08/2014	Inv 13608	4029.75		13463.01
27/08/2014	Credit Note CN259		161.19	13301.82

TOTAL AMOUNT OUTSTANDING **13301.82**

Just the total amounts on the invoices are shown in the statement as the customer will only want to know what he owes. What part is VAT and how much the trade discount is, is shown on the invoice and is irrelevant here.

Chapter Summary

Businesses produce a number of documents to keep track of their sales. These documents include:

1. Quotes and estimates
2. Purchase orders
3. Delivery notes
4. Invoices
5. Returns notes
6. Credit Notes
7. Customer statements

VAT is charged on goods and services supplied at the rate of 20%.

If discounts are offered the VAT should be calculated on the reduced amount.

Special rules apply to VAT when a settlement discount is offered.

A credit note should still reflect any settlement discount so that the credit matches the sale.

CHAPTER 2
Selling Goods and Services

Practice Questions

Chapter 2

2.1

What type of document would you use:

a) As a formal notification as to the amount owed?

b) As a reminder to a customer how much is owed?

c) As a formal document to inform the customer how much you intend to charge for the goods or services should the customer accept?

d) To order goods from a supplier?

e) To accompany goods delivered to the buyer?

f) To accompany faulty goods returned to the seller?

g) As a formal document to inform the customer that a refund is to be made for faulty goods?

2.2

What do the following terms mean:

a) E&OE

b) Ex-works

c) COD?

CHAPTER 2
Selling Goods and Services

2.3

T&T sells tiles. This month there is a special offer. If you buy 20 boxes or more a discount of 30% is offered.

The most popular line in tiles is normally offered at £35.00 per box

The following credit customers buy this popular line during the month:

a) D Barton buys 50 boxes
b) E Woodward buys 15 boxes
c) Goodwin Tiles Ltd buys 1000 boxes.

Calculate in each case:

1. The total cost before discount and VAT
2. The discount
3. The cost after discount
4. The VAT charged (current rate 20%)
5. The total cost

2.4

Recalculate the amounts if a 3% settlement discount is offered.

2.5

In the above cases how much would each customer actually pay if the settlement discount were taken?

2.6

F Blake bought some of these tiles before the special offer began. However, he was offered a 3% settlement discount when he ordered them. T&T allows a credit note to all customers who return unopened boxes. F Blake is now returning 10 boxes for a refund.

Calculate:

a) The total amount of the refund before VAT
b) The VAT amount refunded
c) The total amount shown on the Credit Note

2.7

At the beginning November 2014 G Stephens had an opening balance of £325.50.

On 6th November he bought goods worth £650.00 including VAT. (Invoice 23469).

On 7th November he paid £317.00 which was for the opening balance, but which he took £8.50 settlement discount to which he was entitled.

On 21st November he bought more goods worth £700.00 including VAT (Invoice 23576).

On 22nd November he returned goods which were faulty. The value including VAT was £50.00. (Credit Note CN57)

Draw up G Stephen's statement of account for 30th November

STATEMENT OF ACCOUNT

T&T Ltd

154 Margaret St, Immingham, IM17 9RQ

To

G Stephens
65 Dudley Road
Birmingham
B5 4BL

Account GS01

Date

Date	Details	Debit £	Credit £	Balance £

TOTAL AMOUNT OUTSTANDING

Chapter 3

VAT and Legal Considerations

> In this chapter we will cover a basic understanding of how VAT works.
>
> We will also look at some of the legal aspects involved with sales.
>
> You will learn the importance of checking and authorising documents.

Value Added Tax (VAT) is a tax on buying and selling and, along with income tax, is the most important way the government gets its income. Businesses registered for VAT must charge the tax on all the goods they sell (with a few exceptions which are covered in the Indirect Tax Unit of the AAT level 3 Diploma). The rate in the UK is currently 20%.

The first country to adopt VAT on a large scale was France in 1954. Before that a purchase tax was levied which repeatedly taxed a product at every stage of production without relief on the tax already paid. This made goods which were bought and sold several times for each stage of production, artificially high. VAT on the other hand is a tax only on the final consumer (as we shall see in a moment).

A requirement of joining the European Union is that each member state implements VAT broadly based on rules set up by the European Union itself. Standard rates vary between 15% (Luxembourg) to 27% (Hungary), but the process is the same in each country.

In this book we are only going to look at the rates and exemptions which apply in the UK.

When a business reaches (or is expected to reach) a turnover (i.e. total value of all sales in a year) of £79,000, then that business must register for VAT. You will face a penalty of up to 15% of the tax due if you don't. The limit of £79,000 changes more or less each year but this figure is correct for the 2013/14 Financial Year. (If you want to check the current threshold level visit http://www.hmrc.gov.uk/vat/start/register/when-to-register.htm). A business may voluntarily register for VAT before it reaches this limit. Volunteering to charge tax on sales does seem strange at first, but the reason is that VAT registered companies can claim back all the VAT they have paid on goods and services to do with the business. This not only applies to the goods they are going to sell on as part of their trade, but also to all incidental costs and equipment bought, such as computers for the office, stationery and even cleaning products. It is up to each company to consider the advantages and disadvantages of voluntary registration.

CHAPTER 3
VAT and Legal Considerations

Once a company has registered for VAT it will be given a VAT registration number. This number must be quoted on all invoices and credit notes as well as some other business documents. The invoices and credit notes must contain certain information such as the rate of VAT and the total amount of VAT charged (but this will be covered in the Indirect Tax Unit of the AAT level 3 Diploma). For now you will need to know that VAT **must** be charged at the required rate and that it is the **supplier's responsibility** to calculate it correctly.

In simple terms, a VAT registered company will charge VAT on all its sales. This is called **output tax**. The company will pay VAT on all its purchases. This is called **input tax**. Usually a company works out the difference between the output tax and the input tax every three months. If the output tax is more than the input tax then the company pays the difference to HMRC. If the input tax is more than the output tax then the company will receive a refund of the difference from HMRC. To show what inputs and outputs there are, a VAT return (known as **form VAT 100**) is sent to HMRC quarterly. In most cases this must now be completed online. There are other schemes such as the annual accounting scheme and the cash accounting scheme, but these will be covered in the Indirect Tax Unit of the AAT level 3 Diploma.

A lower rate of 5% is applied to certain products. These include domestic fuel, women's sanitary products, children's car seats and contraceptives.

Some goods are set at zero rate. This includes food (but not confectionary, nor to food in restaurants or hot takeaways), books, children's clothes and public transport (provided it is designed to carry 10 passengers or more).

A number of items are exempt from VAT. You must make sure you understand the difference between zero rated and exempt sales. If you make zero rated sales then you can still claim back all the input VAT. If on the other hand you make exempt sales then you **cannot reclaim** any VAT. Exempt items include betting, burial and cremation, education (in certain circumstances), health (such as doctors' or hospital costs), land and new buildings for private dwelling, and postal services by the Post Office.

EXAM ALERT!

You must know the difference between exempt and zero rated sales for VAT purposes. If you make zero rated sales you can claim back any input VAT. If you make only exempt sales you can't.

Let us now take a look at how VAT is only a tax on the final consumer. We will use an example of making a cabinet for sale of £300 plus VAT. VAT at 20% on £300 is £60.00.

CHAPTER 3
VAT and Legal Considerations

The following example shows how HMRC only collects £60.00 even though there are four stages to the sale, each of which involves VAT.

WOOD SUPPLIER

The wood supplier sells the wood to the manufacturer for £150.00. He/she charges £150.00 plus £30.00 VAT. The wood supplier will collect £180.00. He keeps £150.00 and sends £30.00 to HMRC.

↓

MANUFACTURER

The Manufacturer buys the wood for £150.00 plus £30.00 VAT. He/she adds on his profit margin and sells the cabinet to the shop for £240.00 plus £48.00 VAT. The manufacturer collects £288.00. He/she keeps £240.00 for him/herself and owes £48.00 to HMRC but remember that he/she has already paid £30.00 in VAT to the wood supplier. The manufacturer calculates that the difference between the input VAT and the output VAT is (£48.00 - £30.00 =) £18.00. The manufacturer pays £18.00 to HMRC.

↓

SHOP

The shop buys the cabinet for £240.00 plus £48.00. The shopkeeper adds on a profit margin and sells the cabinet to the final customer for £300 plus £60.00 VAT. The shop keeper collects £360.00. He/she keeps £300.00 for him/herself and owes £60.00 to HMRC but remember that he/she has already paid £48.00 VAT for the cabinet to the manufacturer. The shop keeper calculates that the difference between the input VAT and the output VAT is (£60.00 - £48.00 =) £12.00. The shop keeper pays £12.00 to HMRC.

↓

FINAL CUSTOMER

The final customer buys the cabinet for £300.00 plus £60.00. He/she cannot claim back any VAT so he/she has to pay £360.00 to the shopkeeper. He/she pays nothing directly to HMRC.

SUMMING UP

The wood supplier pays £30.00 to HMRC	£30.00
The manufacturer pays £18.00 to HMRC	£18.00
The shop keeper pays £12.00 to HMRC	£12.00
The final customer pays £0.00 to HMRC	£ 0.00
TOTAL TO HMRC	**£60.00**
VAT CHARGED TO FINAL CUSTOMER	**£60.00**

Readers should now see that the only person to actually pay any VAT is the final customer even though the actual payments have been made in various amounts by the people supplying the goods.

VAT officers are responsible for the collection of VAT for the government. They visit businesses to make sure that their VAT records are up to date. They will need to look at all the sales and purchase invoices along with your VAT account which is a separate record you must keep of the VAT you charged on your sales and the VAT you paid on your purchases. You must keep all these records for **six** years.

You should remember that when you calculate the VAT amount to charge your customer, if the amount doesn't work out to whole pence, there are different rounding rules. For invoices between VAT registered businesses the rule is to round down.

VAT ROUNDING

Suppose we are selling goods to a value of £104.59.

Calculate the VAT on this amount
£104.59 x 20% (or 20 / 100) = £20.918

Obviously we cannot charge a customer 0.8p so (unlike normal mathematical rules) we just ignore the extra amount over and above the penny. The amount of VAT to charge is £20.91

You need to be able to do one final calculation when it comes to VAT. Suppose you buy goods which simply states that the price includes VAT. On amounts below £250.00 you don't require such a detailed invoice and the VAT is not split out like on the more detailed invoices. Let's look at the calculation for this.

Calculating the VAT amount from a gross amount

The total of an invoice (or till receipt) is the **gross** amount. It will often include VAT. The amount shown is the 100% of the goods value plus 20% being the VAT amount. The gross amount is therefore 120%.

Let us suppose our invoice show a gross amount of £147.00.

Divide £147.00 by 120 = 1.225

Multiply 1.225 by 20 to arrive at the VAT amount = £24.50. If the answer doesn't come to a whole penny remember that you will need to round DOWN.

Remember that if you multiply the 1.225 by 100 you will arrive at the net amount of the goods which in this case will be £122.50.

WARNING – You cannot find the amount of VAT from the gross amount by calculating 20% of it. If you tried to do this in the above example you would find that £147.00 x 20% comes to £29.40. This is a long way from the correct answer.

CHAPTER 3
VAT and Legal Considerations

Legal aspects of sales and purchases

LEARNING POINT

The legal aspects of sales and purchases will not be assessed in the 'Processing Bookkeeping Transactions' exam or the 'Control Accounts, Journals and the Banking System' exam. This section is here to give supplementary knowledge of the regulations relating to sales, purchases and contracts

Every time we make a sale or buy something from a shop we are entering into a contract. The simple act of buying a cup of coffee from the café means that you have entered into a contract.

A contract is a legally binding agreement enforceable by law. Contrary to popular belief, a contract does not have to be in writing (although some items must be in writing such as the transfer of land). In fact, some contracts don't even need to be spoken; they can be implied. For example, if you go to the opticians for an eye test, you will expect to pay a fair price. If you refuse to pay you will be in breach of contract.

For a contract to exist there must be three elements:

1. **Agreement**. One person (called a party in legal jargon) must make an offer and another must accept
2. **Consideration**. Each party must promise to do or give something to the other. (In the case of buying goods one party will give the goods in return for payment)
3. **Intention to create legal relations.** Each party must have had the intention that the contract should be legally binding. (You can't sue your friend for not buying you dinner as there was no intention that the agreement should be legally binding)

In addition, a contract can only be made if:

The parties have the capacity to enter into the agreement. Minors (people under the age of 18), bankrupts, people with mental incompetence, and intoxicated persons cannot form a contract.
The agreement must have been entered into freely. A contract cannot be legally binding if one or both parties have been pressured or influenced into making the contract.
The agreement must be legal. For instance, you can't form a contract to buy and sell illegal drugs. Similarly you cannot contract a person to carry out a robbery.

Let us look at what an **offer and an acceptance** is in legal terms.

CHAPTER 3
VAT and Legal Considerations

An offer is a clear indication that a person is willing to enter into a contract once the offer has been accepted. The offer may be in writing (such as a quote) or it may be verbal or even by conduct. In the supermarket you make the offer by placing the goods on the conveyor.

You must be careful not to confuse an offer with an **invitation to treat**. Goods on the supermarket shelves indicating the price is **not** an offer. It is simply an invitation for someone to make an offer to buy the goods at the price indicated. When it comes to the checkout, the shop is not bound to sell them at the price indicated. Advertisements in the paper are also invitations to treat. Let us take an example of a new computer advertised in the paper for £50. You go straight to the shop and offer to buy the computer for £50. If the shopkeeper refuses to sell you it at £50 saying there was an error in the advertisement, you cannot force them to do so. The advertisement was simply an invitation to treat and not an offer.

For an offer to be accepted it must be accepted unqualified (exactly as agreed) and must be clearly communicated to the person making the offer. If the offer is qualified (altered in any way) then this is a counter-offer. So if you say you will buy the goods as long as it can be delivered in 7 days then there is no acceptance and a contract does not exist.

The acceptance must be firm and clear, but it doesn't have to be in writing. If we go back to the supermarket example, the acceptance takes place when the person at the counter rings it through the till.

An acceptance cannot be assumed by silence. The person making the offer cannot say that he/she will assume you have accepted the offer if he/she doesn't hear from you in 7 days. If that is the case then no contract will be formed.

If the acceptance is by post then the contract is made when the letter is posted (not when it is received by the other party). It may seem unfair, but if the letter is lost in the post then a contract still exists. In contrast, an offer by post is made when the other party receives it.

Now we will look at the **consideration**.

For a contract to exist there must be a **bargain**. Probably a bargain to you means 'a good deal'. In legal terms it is the agreement to pass something of value between parties. Each party in a contract must promise to give something of value to the other. In ordinary sales the supplier will promise the goods while the buyer will promise to pay for them. The 'something of value' is called the 'consideration'. If a neighbour offers to mow your lawn for free then there is no contract since there is no consideration from one of the parties.

The consideration need not be money (you can offer to **do** something in return). It doesn't have to even be a benefit. A neighbour could offer to pay you £10 for not practicing your drum kit after 8 p.m. The consideration is you not playing your drum kit after this time.

The consideration must not be past. This means that if your neighbour mows your lawn and then next week you offer to pay him/her £10, then there is no contract since mowing the lawn had already taken place before you offered to pay.

Consideration must be sufficient but need not be adequate. This phrase simply means that the consideration must be of value although it may not be adequate. For example, if you sell your car for £1, your money is of value so there is a contract, even though the £1 may not be seen as adequate value for the car.

The consideration must move from the promisee. The promisee is the person who has been promised the goods or service and the phrase means that it is the promisee who should provide the consideration. If you agree to pay for goods and your friend actually pays for them then a contract does not exist.

The intention to create legal relations may seem difficult to prove, but in general the law divides agreements into two groups. Social and domestic agreements cover agreements between family, friends and workmates. Unless it can be proved otherwise, such agreements are considered not to be legally binding. In contrast, business agreements are considered to have legal intent, although this can be overturned by the terms of the contract. It is important to read the 'small print'. In 1938 there was a law suit (Jones v Vernon Pools) whereby Jones claimed to have won the pools. The coupon stated that the transaction was "binding in honour only". It was held that Jones was not entitled to recover because the agreement was based on the honour of the parties (and thus not legally binding).

A contract is considered to be **discharged** (completed and no longer binding) in the following circumstances:

1. **Performance**. This is when both parties have carried out the terms of the contract in full and to the satisfaction of the other party.
2. **Agreement**. The two parties can agree not to carry out the contract. For example, suppose you get someone to decorate your dining room. You agree to pay the decorator on completion but he/she doesn't turn up. You can agree with the decorator to abandon the work, in which case the contract will be discharged.
3. **Frustration**. A contract is frustrated if it becomes impossible to perform. Let us suppose that you contract a builder to build you a conservatory. Once the foundations have been dug it becomes apparent that the land is not stable enough to support any kind of building. The contract is frustrated as the contract has become impossible to fulfil. In this case the contract would be discharged.
4. **Breach of contract**. This is where there is a failure to carry out the terms of the contract. The terms may be written in the contract or they may be implied. For example, when you buy goods you should expect them to be of satisfactory quality even though this is not written in the contract.

CHAPTER 3
VAT and Legal Considerations

Statute Law

A statute is a formal, written law of a country or state. There are three main UK statute laws to do with buying and selling:

> **The Sale of Goods Act 1979 (as amended)**
> **The Trades Description Act 1968 (as amended)**
> **The Unfair Contract Terms Act 1977**

The **Sale of Goods Act** lays down conditions that all goods sold by a trader must meet. The goods must be:

> **As described**. This includes not only the written description but also any verbal description given at the time. If you are told that a skirt is made of pure silk, then it must be made of silk and not imitation.
>
> **Of satisfactory quality.** Goods are of satisfactory quality if they reach the standard that a reasonable person would regard as satisfactory, taking into account the price and any description. It covers minor defects such as scratches and blemishes as well as more serious defects unless the buyer was made aware of the defect at the time. It also means that the goods should last a reasonable length of time. If you buy a watch and it stops after a few weeks then it is not of satisfactory quality and you are entitled to a refund.
>
> **Fit for purpose**. This covers not only what the goods are supposed to do but also any assurances given to the customer. If you buy a computer program and you specify that it will be for use with a certain operating system, and subsequently find that it does not work on this system, then you will have a right to a refund.

A seller cannot pass on the responsibility for faulty goods to the manufacturer. The contract is between the seller and the buyer, and as such the responsibility for faulty goods lies with the seller.

A shop cannot overcome the Sale of Goods Act by any terms of contract or by signs in the shop. A customer's rights are not altered by signs saying 'No refunds'. However, a customer cannot demand a refund simply because he/she has changed his/her mind. It is also not true that you have to produce a receipt in order to get your money back, but it is reasonable for the shopkeeper to have some assurance that the goods were bought from him/her. A cheque stub or credit card statement should be sufficient.

The fact that goods were in a sale does not mean that the seller's responsibilities can be waived, although it is likely that any faults or problems would be obvious to the customer. A customer cannot demand money back if the faults were known to him/her at the time of purchase.

An important point to note is that as a trader, you don't have completely the same rights as a consumer (i.e. someone who is not buying in the course of business). If you are a consumer, in place of a refund, you can ask for a repair or replacement.

CHAPTER 3
VAT and Legal Considerations

The Trades Description Act requires that any descriptions of goods and services, given by a person acting in the course of a trade or business, should be accurate and not misleading. A description not only applies to physical description, but also to the history of the goods (e.g. used to belong to Elton John, or previously advertised at £100) or that it is approved by a professional body (e.g. AAT approved). You cannot say that you are a chartered accountant if you are not.

Anyone selling the goods can be guilty of an offence under the Act, including directors and all levels of employees. The Act provides for a defence if the seller can prove that the information about the goods was made by relying on information supplied to him/her, but the seller must also prove that all reasonable steps were made to avoid giving false information.

The maximum penalty for offences under the Act is two years' imprisonment and an unlimited fine.

The Unfair Contract Terms Act puts some restrictions on the 'small print' that can be put into a contract. In general, businesses are allowed to make whatever agreements they like, but a business is not allowed to use an exclusion clause which excludes liability for death or injury. Clauses excluding liability for defective goods can only be enforceable if it is 'reasonable'. What is 'reasonable' will ultimately be decided by the courts.

At present there are separate rules covering unfair **consumer** contracts; the Unfair Terms in Consumer Contracts Regulations. An exclusion clause for defective goods would automatically not be allowed in a consumer contract. However, you should be aware that a sole trader is considered a business in relation to this Act.

Authorising and checking documentation

As part of a business's control system, all documents and letters sent to customers should be checked and in some instances authorised before they are sent. Accuracy in accounting is essential as mistakes can cost money. As you have seen above, once you have made your contract you can't go back on it, so if you get your quote wrong, or draw up an incorrect invoice you could be stuck with it.

To check that an invoice is correct you should refer to the purchase order. You should check:

> The customer is correct. (You may have customers with similar names such as J Smith and T Smith).
> The goods are correct and at the correct price. Often goods will have a product code which will make it easier to check. You can match the price with your own company's catalogue or stock record.
> The quantity is correct. Expensive mistakes could be made if the purchase order says 50 units and you send 500.

Has the correct rate of any discount been applied? You can usually find this out from the customer records.
Are the calculations correct particularly with the VAT? Remember it is the responsibility of the supplier to get this right.

Of course, if your company uses a computer package to raise invoices then much of the above will be done automatically. Nevertheless, you still need to check codes such as product codes, customer codes and purchase order numbers. Your computer package will only calculate on the basis of the data you input, so if your input is wrong then the computer will get its output wrong.

Most customers will have a credit limit. This is the limit at which they will be supplied goods on credit. While it is not impossible to supply the goods above the credit limit, any invoices taking the amount above the limit will need to be authorised by a more senior person. You should never supply goods to a customer without the proper authorisation.

Other documents will also need authorisation, particularly Purchase Orders and Credit Notes. Purchases need authorisation to avoid purchasing too much stock, and anything to do with returning goods should be authorised to avoid customers claiming money for returned goods to which they are not entitled.

Chapter Summary

VAT between businesses is always rounded down to the nearest penny.

The VAT amount can be calculated from the gross amount.

A contract is formed when goods are bought and sold. There are legal terms and regulations in forming a contract.

Statutory law covers some aspects of selling.

Documents relating to sales must be checked and in some cases authorised by a more senior person.

CHAPTER 3
VAT and Legal Considerations

Practice Questions

Chapter 3

3.1

The following amounts include VAT. In each case what is the amount of VAT included in the total. (Remember that you must round down to the nearest penny).

a) £210.00
b) £0.42
c) £1.74
d) £18,192.18
e) £335.72

3.2

What are the 3 elements of a contract?

3.3

You see an advertisement in the local paper for a new cooker. It says 'One only – Cookmaster cooker – only £150.00'. You rush to the store to buy the cooker but are told that the advertisement should have read £350.00. Can you insist on the price of £150? Give reasons for your answer.

3.4

You order a games console for your son's birthday through a mail order catalogue. Your son's birthday is 2 weeks away, but the order form says delivery may take up to 28 days. At the bottom of your order form you write in big letters, 'order placed on the basis I will receive it within 2 weeks'. Does a contract exist?

3.5

Your elderly neighbour has a garden. You know that she finds it difficult to keep her garden in trim so you offer to cut her grass and prune her roses free of charge. A few days later she comes to your door with £10 as a thank you for doing the garden. Unfortunately her prized rose bushes die and she claims that they died because you didn't prune them properly. Did a contract exist and so does she have a case in law against you?

3.6

You buy a watch in the sale. It has been reduced from £100 to £40. It looks like a real bargain so you buy the watch. One week later the watch stops and it is impossible to get it going again, so you take it back to the shop for a refund. The shopkeeper refuses saying it was in the sale and so no refunds can be given. Is the shopkeeper right?

3.7

You buy a new monitor for your computer. It is advertised as having an adjustable stand 'for comfort of viewing'. When you get it home you find that the stand is not adjustable at all. You take it back for a refund, but the shopkeeper refuses because he says you saw it wasn't adjustable when you took it. Is the shopkeeper right?

3.8

You buy a shirt which is packaged as a 15 inch collar. When you get it home the size on the garment says 18 inch collar and it doesn't fit properly. You take it back to the shop and ask for a refund, but you have lost the receipt. However, the shirt has the shop's name on a label and you have the credit card statement as proof of purchase. The shopkeeper points to a sign saying 'no refunds without a receipt' and she says it is more than her job is worth than to refund without a receipt. Is the shopkeeper right?

3.9

List four ways a contract may be discharged.

3.10

A customer asks if you can supply a particular type of musical keyboard in time for Christmas. These keyboards are hard to come by. You find a supplier who has one and it is duly ordered. You tell the customer it will arrive by the end of the week. Unfortunately, when it arrives there is an electrical fault and it doesn't work. You ask your supplier for a replacement or a repair. The supplier says he will give a refund but cannot replace or repair. Is the supplier within his rights to do this?

Chapter 4

Recording Sales and Sales Returns

In this chapter we will be looking at how we record a credit sale in our books.

We will look at recording sales returns.

We shall see how the documents shown in Chapter 2 are recorded in the books of prime entry and then into the double entry accounts.

We shall look at the uses of a Sales Ledger Control account and how to reconcile it.

We shall learn how to balance an account.

Some very small businesses will only keep a record of receipts and payments. This method of recording each transaction once is called **single entry** bookkeeping. While it is useful for showing net income (the difference between the total value of receipts and payments) it is not very useful for showing the financial position of a company. It doesn't show the value of the company, what its assets are and what its liabilities are. It doesn't show what is owed and what is owned.

For this reason many businesses use a more sophisticated method of recording transactions. This is the **double entry** system. The principle is that each transaction has a double effect. If we record a sale for example, then our cash will increase but our stock will decrease. Using the double entry system each transaction will be recorded twice. The transactions are recorded into **accounts**. There will be an account for each type of transaction, so there will be a sales account, a purchases account, an account for each type of expense, as well as an account for each customer who buys goods on credit. All these accounts together are known as the **integrated ledger**. However, you can see that some businesses will have so many accounts that it becomes unmanageable just as one ledger, so it will be divided up. You will come across:

Sales ledger - recording all the transactions with your credit customers. It will show what your customers owe you. (It doesn't record cash sales).
Purchases ledger - recording all the transactions with your credit suppliers. It will show what you owe your suppliers. (It also doesn't record cash sales).
Cash book – recording all the cash **and bank** transaction. (You must remember to include bank transactions here in spite of it being called a 'cash book')
Main ledger – records all the other transactions such as expenses, loans, money you have put into the business and money you have taken out, any equipment you

have bought for the business. The main ledger is also known as the 'general' ledger or the 'nominal' ledger.

Credit sales

So let us look how we get from the invoice which was raised to the records in our accounts.

The first thing to understand is that a 'sale' in accounting means a sale of goods the business usually trades in. If your company sells clothes then you cannot count the sale of your old computer as a sale in the accounts. This will be recorded separately. (You will see how to do this in detail later in your studies). So firstly you will have to ensure that the invoice you are recording as a sale can be classed as such.

The invoices will first be recorded in a **Sales Day Book**. It is called a day book because this is where sales are recorded on a daily basis. This is the **book of prime entry** used for sales. It is called a book of prime entry as this is where the invoice is recorded first.

SALES DAY BOOK **SDB 15**

Date	Invoice	Customer	Folio	Total		Sales Clothes		Sales Fabrics		VAT	
2014				£	p	£	p	£	p	£	p
04 Aug	3695	G Hall	SL 28	350	95	350	95				
11 Aug	3696	H Lewis	SL 31	425	62	425	62				
18 Aug	3697	I Harris	SL 29	321	56			321	56		
26 Aug	3698	J Clarke	SL 06	259	85			259	85		
27 Aug	3699	K Khan	SL 42	329	75	329	75				
31 Aug		**TOTAL FOR THE MONTH**		**1687**	**73**	**1106**	**32**	**581**	**41**		

CHAPTER 4
Recording Sales and Sales Returns

Let us look in detail what the Sales Day Book has in it.

SDB 15. This is the reference number of the page of the Sales Day Book. So that we can refer to this page in other parts of the ledgers this number will be used as a cross reference. (SDB stands for Sales Day Book, but other code numbers can be found in use).
The date. This is the date the invoice was raised.
The invoice number. These must be in sequence. If a number is missing then there is an invoice missing. The fact that the invoices are numbered sequentially is a check to ensure that all invoices have been recorded. In a manual system where invoices are raised by hand, if an invoice has been spoiled then it should be recorded as such in the Sales Day Book.
The name of the customer. If it is a credit sale then you will know the name of the customer. Remember that only credit sales are recorded in the Sales Day Book.
The folio. This is the cross-reference code. You will need to record the invoice in the customer account in the Sales Ledger. SL stands for Sales Ledger and the number is the page on which this customer can be found. If you're using a computer then the code may well be letters and numbers (alpha-numeric) which represent each customer.
The total amount. This is the total amount of the invoice. In this example we have assumed that the company is not registered for VAT. We will look at how to deal with VAT later in this chapter.
There are two columns for sales. Some companies are interested in what they have sold and categorise them. Obviously if this is not of concern to the company then only one column will be used.
Since our company is not registered for VAT the VAT column will be left blank.
The Sales Day Book is totalled at regular intervals. It will depend on each company whether this is daily, weekly or monthly. In this case it is monthly.
You can check that your adding up is correct as the monthly overall total will equal the total of the other columns (£581.41 + £1106.32 = £1687.73).

So now we can transfer the amounts shown in the Sales Day Book to the ledger accounts.

An account in a manual system usually takes a whole page and each account is split into two. A line is drawn down the middle. On the left are **debits** and on the right are **credits**. Debit is often shortened to DR and credit is shortened to CR. The abbreviations come from the Latin; *debere* means to be indebted, and *credere* means to loan. The use of 'debit' and 'credit' is merely to distinguish which side of the account you are referring to. The problem is that most people get their idea of what is a debit and what is a credit from their bank account. If you are in credit at the bank then it usually means you have funds in the bank (i.e. you're not overdrawn). Your bank statement even shows it like this with withdrawals on the left (the debit side) and deposits on the right (the credit side). In actual fact, for you the customer, this is the wrong way round. The point is that the bank is showing things from their own point of view and not yours so everything is reversed.

From your own personal point of view, deposits into the bank are debits on the left hand side and withdrawals are credits on the right hand side.

> **LEARNING POINT**
>
> Debits and Credits is one of the most difficult concepts to learn. Even well established accounting technicians still get it wrong. As a starting point you should look on debits as receiving and credits as giving.

One of the principles of double entry bookkeeping is that the total of all debits should equal the total of all credits. So whatever figure you put into the debits you must also put into the credits.

Let us take the first invoice from the Sales Day Book (see p 48).

G Hall's invoice is for £350.95. This amount is a request for the customer to pay the amount shown. In other words it is an amount that your company will receive. As it is an amount we will receive it will be shown as a debit in the customer's account.

Each account is shown in the form of a 'T'. You will therefore often hear them referred to as **'T' accounts**.

Dr	**G Hall Account**	Cr

You will find the name of the account at the top along with Dr on the left and Cr on the right.

So now let's put the first entry into the account. Remember that we are only entering the amount on the debit (left) side as it is the receiving part of the double entry. We'll need:

Date (of the transaction).
Details (some idea where the figure came from. This will either be the book of prime entry or it may indicate the account where the other half of the double entry has been made).
The amount.

Dr		G Hall Account			Cr
Date	Details	£	Date	Details	£
04/08/14	SDB 15	350.95			

Now let us look at the other side of the double entry.

The 'giving' side of the transaction is the sale. It is the giving of the goods. We must find the sales account in the main ledger and credit that account with the amount of the invoice.

Dr		Sales Account (Clothes)			Cr
Date	Details	£	Date	Details	£
			04/08/14	SDB 15	350.95

We have now recorded our first double entry transaction. To make things simpler we might just enter all the invoices in the customer accounts and then simply put the totals in the Sales Account. In our case you would have two sales accounts. You would need to credit the Sales Account (Clothes) with £1106.32 and credit the Sales Account (Fabrics) with £581.41. Each customer account would of course have its own invoices as debits. The main point is that you ensure that the total of the debits equals the total of the credits.

Of course, if you use a computer program much of this will be done for you, but the principle is the same. Computer programs will also require the accounts to be coded, so the customer account could well be H001 and the sales account might be 4000.

EXAM ALERT!

You **will** be expected to be able to record sales in the double entry system. If you're not completely sure, go back and revise this section again. Understanding this is the basis of **all** the topics you will cover in financial accounting.

Now let's try something slightly more complex. We will carry out the same sales, but this time we will assume that your company **is** registered for VAT.

We will start with the Sales Day Book as before.

SALES DAY BOOK **SDB 15**

Date	Invoice	Customer	Folio	Total		Sales Clothes		Sales Fabrics		VAT	
2014				£	p	£	p	£	p	£	p
04 Aug	3695	G Hall	SL 28	421	14	350	95			70	19
11 Aug	3696	H Lewis	SL 31	510	74	425	62			85	12
18 Aug	3697	I Harris	SL 29	385	87			321	56	64	31
26 Aug	3698	J Clarke	SL 06	311	82			259	85	51	97
27 Aug	3699	K Khan	SL 42	395	70	329	75			65	95
31 Aug		**TOTAL FOR THE MONTH**		**2025**	**27**	**1106**	**32**	**581**	**41**	**337**	**54**

The first thing you will notice is that the figures in the Sales columns haven't changed. The only thing that has changed is the VAT which has pushed up the price on each invoice and so the total figure for all the invoices. What you have to remember is that you are selling goods and not VAT. You are just collecting the VAT for HMRC.

As before, if you add up the two sales columns and the VAT columns it will come to the invoice total column (£337.54 + £581.41 + £1106.32 = £2025.27). You should get used to doing this check as it saves problems later.

So now let us look at entering the first invoice as before into the accounts.

This time we will enter the total amount into the customer account. This is because this is the total amount he owes us. We are not interested in this account how much he owes us for VAT and how much for the goods separately. This information will be shown elsewhere in the ledgers.

Dr		**G Hall Account**			Cr
Date	Details	£	Date	Details	£
04/08/14	SDB 15	421.14			
	(alternatively				
	you can use				
	the invoice				
	number)				

The other 'half' of the double entry will now have to be in two parts. We need to record the sale and then we need to record the VAT. We can't record the VAT along with the sale or we would look like we were selling goods **and** VAT.

Dr		**Sales Account (Clothes)**			Cr
Date	Details	£	Date	Details	£
			04/08/14	SDB 15	350.95

You will notice that the Sales Account is no different at all than in the previous example. However, the debits don't match the credits, so we need to put in an extra amount somewhere. You will need a VAT account (sometimes referred to as a VAT control account). A VAT control account tracks the amount of VAT payable and reclaimable by a business.

Dr		**VAT Account**			Cr
Date	Details	£	Date	Details	£
			04/08/14	SDB 15	70.19

Again it is more common (and saves time) to simply enter the total figures for the Sales and VAT rather than entering them one at a time.

CHAPTER 4

Recording Sales and Sales Returns

Let us now look at the complete set of accounts to record the invoices from the Sales Day Book. To save space, (as is typical in exams and exercises), we will not use a whole page for each account.

SALES LEDGER

Dr		**G Hall Account**			Cr
Date	Details	£	Date	Details	£
04/08/14	SDB 15	421.14			

Dr		**H Lewis Account**			Cr
Date	Details	£	Date	Details	£
11/08/14	SDB 15	510.74			

Dr		**I Harris Account**			Cr
Date	Details	£	Date	Details	£
18/08/14	SDB 15	385.87			

Dr		**J Clarke Account**			Cr
Date	Details	£	Date	Details	£
26/08/14	SDB 15	311.82			

Dr		**K Khan Account**			Cr
Date	Details	£	Date	Details	£
27/08/14	SDB 15	395.70			

MAIN LEDGER

Dr			Sales Account (Clothes)		Cr
Date	Details	£	Date	Details	£
			31/08/14	SDB 15	1106.32

Dr			Sales Account (Fabrics)		Cr
Date	Details	£	Date	Details	£
			31/08/14	SDB 15	581.41

Dr			VAT Account		Cr
Date	Details	£	Date	Details	£
			31/08/14	SDB 15	337.54

Notice that the Sales Accounts and the VAT account have only the total amounts and not each individual amount. We are only interested in how much sales we have made and how much VAT we owe to HMRC. However, in the individual customer accounts we would want to see each individual transaction. In case of query the customer account is the first place we would look.

Now if you add up all the debits and then add up all the credits you will see that the debit total is the same as the credit total.

You can probably already see that this system can become unwieldy, particularly if management or the owner wants to see how much is owed to the company at any particular time. To make information easier to extract from our accounts there is a system of **control accounts**. Control accounts are summaries of sets of accounts. They are very useful because they get rid of the large amount of detail which is not always required. The detail will still be recorded, but the double entry main ledger will be kept clear of clutter.

In our example above you can see that, if we want to know how much is owed to us by credit customers, we would have to add up all the totals from the Sales Ledger each time this information was required. To get round this inconvenience we need to draw up a **Sales Ledger Control Account**. The Sales Ledger Control account will only contain a summary of the Sales Ledger. (Think of the word 'control' meaning 'summary').

This will mean a little reorganisation of our accounts. Each individual customer account will **not** now be part of the double entry. Instead, a **Subsidiary Sales Ledger** will contain these accounts. The double entry will be made in the Sales Ledger Control instead.

Let us look how a Sales Ledger Control account would affect our example for sales.

The Sales Ledger would look exactly the same except that now it would **not** be part of the double entry. The main ledger would now have an extra account – the Sales Ledger Control.

MAIN LEDGER

Dr		**Sales Account (Clothes)**			Cr
Date	Details	£	Date	Details	£
			31/08/14	SDB 15	1106.32

Dr		**Sales Account (Fabrics)**			Cr
Date	Details	£	Date	Details	£
			31/08/14	SDB 15	581.41

Dr		**VAT Account**			Cr
Date	Details	£	Date	Details	£
			31/08/14	SDB 15	337.54

Dr		**Sales Ledger Control Account**			Cr
Date	Details	£	Date	Details	£
31/08/14	SDB 15	2025.27			

You can see how just the total from the Sales Day Book is entered in the Sales Ledger Control account, but the total of the debits and the total of the credits will still be the same.

It is now easier for different departments to use the accounts separately. For example, those departments dealing with customer accounts (such as credit control) can use the detail contained in the Subsidiary Sales Ledger, while those involved with the total financial records of the company can use the Main Ledger, free of the detail of each customer. Remember that in the customer accounts you should enter each transaction separately, but in the Sales Ledger Control you should enter just the total figure.

The Sales Ledger Control account is also another check that the total amounts for each customer is correct. Each company will **reconcile** the Sales Ledger Control account with the Subsidiary Sales Ledger. ('Reconcile' means 'agree'). How often this is done is up to each individual company. In our example it is monthly.

Let us look at how the Sales Ledger Control account is reconciled.

Reconciliation of Sales Ledger Control Account
31st August 2014

	£	£
G Hall	421.14	
H Lewis	510.74	
I Harris	385.87	
J Clarke	311.82	
K Khan	395.70	
TOTAL	**2025.27**	
TOTAL PER SALES LEDGER CONTROL		**2025.27**
Discrepancy (if any)	nil	

Of course, if there were a discrepancy then you would need to investigate immediately.

EXAM ALERT!

You may be asked to perform a reconciliation **with** a discrepancy. You will then be asked to suggest a reason for the discrepancy. This is usually a figure which has been incorrectly copied, or it may be an invoice which has been omitted from either the Sales Ledger or the Sales Ledger Control account.

One tip to note in spotting errors. If the discrepancy is 9 or a multiple of 9, first check to see if there has been a reversal of figures. For example a 45 may have been written as a 54. You will notice that the difference between these two figures is 9.

Sales returns

We covered Credit Notes in the previous chapter, but now we will learn how to record one in our books. Let us continue with the example of credit sales. If you look at the Sales Day Book on p 52 you will see that G Hall had an invoice for £421.14 and H Lewis had an invoice for £510.74. Suppose that G Hall found a fault in some of the clothes and wants to return some. We agree and send him a credit note for £40.00 plus VAT. Suppose also that H Lewis finds the fault in some of the clothes we sold him. We agree to send him a Credit Note for £120.00 plus VAT.

When we come to write up these credit notes we will start from the copy of the credit notes and enter them into the **Sales Returns Day Book**. Note that we don't alter the Sales Day Book or the sales in any way. This could lead to confusion over what has been sold. Invoices and Credit Notes must be accounted for separately.

You will notice that the Sales Returns Day Book looks almost identical to the Sales Day Book.

SALES RETURNS DAY BOOK **SRDB 02**

Date	Cr Note	Customer	Folio	Total		Sales Clothes		Sales Fabrics		VAT	
2014				£	p	£	p	£	p	£	p
06 Aug	CN52	G Hall	SL 28	48	00	40	00			8	00
13 Aug	CN53	H Lewis	SL 31	144	00	120	00			24	00
31 Aug		**TOTAL FOR THE MONTH**		**192**	**00**	**160**	**00**	**0**	**00**	**32**	**00**

This time the customer accounts will be **credited** as we are 'giving' them their money back.

SALES LEDGER

Dr		G Hall Account			Cr
Date	Details	£	Date	Details	£
04/08/14	SDB 15	421.14	**06/08/14**	**SRDB 02**	**48.00**

Dr		H Lewis Account			Cr
Date	Details	£	Date	Details	£
11/08/14	SDB 15	510.74	**13/08/14**	**SRDB 02**	**144.00**

Dr		**I Harris Account**			Cr
Date	Details	£	Date	Details	£
18/08/14	SDB 15	385.87			

Dr		**J Clarke Account**			Cr
Date	Details	£	Date	Details	£
26/08/14	SDB 15	311.82			

Dr		**K Khan Account**			Cr
Date	Details	£	Date	Details	£
27/08/14	SDB 15	395.70			

The entries here are in bold so you can see what has been done in the customer accounts.

We will assume that the company keeps a Sales Ledger Control account, so the entries we have just made are in the Subsidiary Sales Ledger and do not form part of the double entry. Therefore the double entry in the Main Ledger will look like this.

MAIN LEDGER

Dr		**Sales Account (Clothes)**			Cr
Date	Details	£	Date	Details	£
			31/08/14	SDB 15	1106.32

Dr		**Sales Returns Account (Clothes)**			Cr
Date	Details	£	Date	Details	£
31/08/14	**SRDB 02**	**160.00**			

Dr		**Sales Account (Fabrics)**			Cr
Date	Details	£	Date	Details	£
			31/08/14	SDB 15	581.41

Dr		**Sales Returns Account (Fabrics)**			Cr
Date	Details	£	Date	Details	£

Dr		**VAT Account**			Cr
Date	Details	£	Date	Details	£
31/08/14	**SRDB 02**	**32.00**	31/08/14	SDB 15	337.54

		Sales Ledger Control Account			Cr
Date	Details	£	Date	Details	£
31/08/14	SDB 15	2025.27	**31/08/14**	**SRDB 02**	**192.00**

Again the new entries are in bold.

The first entry is in the Sales Returns account (Clothes). Notice that this is the **net** amount. As has been established before, we are not selling VAT. It is a debit because we are 'receiving' the goods back. You should also notice that the return is put in its own account. Some smaller companies will simply use the Sales account, but most companies, (and almost all companies in your exam) will use a Sales Returns account.

The next entry is in the VAT account. This is the VAT that we now don't have to pay to HMRC. In effect we are 'receiving' the VAT amount due back from the customer.

The third entry, and the one which completes the double entry, is in the Sales Ledger Control. It is a credit entry as, in effect, we are 'giving' the customers their money back, just as it was in the customer accounts in the Subsidiary Sales Ledger.

Just as before, if you now add up all the debits and then all the credits in the main ledger, they should come to the same figure.

LEARNING POINT

Students make more errors by putting the wrong amounts in these accounts than any other type of error. Make sure you know which account to put the **net** amount in and which to put the **gross** amount in.

Balancing accounts

In the previous examples we have only shown a few entries in each account. But imagine if there were dozens of entries on each side of the account. It would not be easy to see the total of each account. For example, if we had a customer who made regular purchases and regular returns it would not be easy to see at a glance how much this customer still owed. With other accounts (such as the VAT account) you need to know whether the balance is a debit or a credit as well as how much, as you need to know if you owe or are owed. For this reason we must **balance** our accounts regularly.

Let us take an imaginary customer account called Morris & Sons

Dr		**Morris & Sons Account**			Cr
Date	Details	£	Date	Details	£
01/08/14	Balance b/d	490.00	04/08/14	Sales Returns	90.00
01/08/14	Sales	500.00	11/08/14	Sales Returns	30.00
08/08/14	Sales	360.00	18/08/14	Sales Returns	45.00
15/08/14	Sales	490.00	25/08/14	Sales Returns	58.00
22/08/14	Sales	560.00			
30/08/14	Sales	620.00			

You can see that the balance on the account from the previous period is £490.00. To see how much Morris & Sons owe us at the end of this period we need to balance the account.

Balancing an Account

1. Total each side of the account. You should include the balance b/d, (brought down from the previous period) but you shouldn't write these figures on the account. You should just make a note of them. In our case the debit side comes to £3020.00 and the credit side comes to £223.00

2. Calculate the difference between the two sides. £3020.00 - £223.00 = £2797.00.

3. Enter this figure on the side with the smaller total as the balance to carry down (Balance c/d). The date should be the last date of the period.

4. A line should be drawn under the figures on each side. The total for each side should now be the same. This total figure should be entered on each side, but most importantly on the same row. Our total figure will be £3020.00.

5. Draw another line (or sometimes a double line) under these column totals. This indicates that the account has now been balanced.

6. We must have a new b/d balance to match the c/d figure entered at point 3 above. The b/d balance will be entered on the **opposite** side to the c/d balance and on the first date of the new period.

Let us now look at how the calculations are put into practice

Dr		**Morris & Sons Account**			Cr
Date	Details	£	Date	Details	£
01/08/14	Balance b/d	490.00	04/08/14	Sales Returns	90.00
01/08/14	Sales	500.00	11/08/14	Sales Returns	30.00
08/08/14	Sales	360.00	18/08/14	Sales Returns	45.00
15/08/14	Sales	490.00	25/08/14	Sales Returns	58.00
22/08/14	Sales	560.00	**31/08/14**	**Balance c/d**	**2797.00**
30/08/14	Sales	620.00			
		3020.00			**3020.00**
01/09/14	**Balance b/d**	**2797.00**			

You should pay particular attention to:

The date of the balance c/d is the last day of the period

That the column totals are underlined, that they are on the same row and that they are the same figure

The balance b/d is on the first day of the new period and is the same as the balance c/d

EXAM ALERT!

Accuracy and clear work are of paramount importance in accounts. Marks are awarded for this in exams.

You are very likely to be asked to balance one or a number of accounts. You must stick to this method if you want to gain the maximum marks.

Now let us return to our example of the clothes and fabric company. Let us balance the accounts which we last showed on pages 59 to 61.

SALES LEDGER

Dr		**G Hall Account**			Cr
Date	Details	£	Date	Details	£
04/08/14	SDB 15	421.14	06/08/14	SRDB 02	48.00
			31/08/14	Balance c/d	373.14
		421.14			421.14
01/09/14	Balance b/d	373.14			

Dr		**H Lewis Account**			Cr
Date	Details	£	Date	Details	£
11/08/14	SDB 15	510.74	13/08/14	SRDB 02	144.00
			31/08/14	Balance c/d	366.74
		510.74			510.74
01/09/14	Balance b/d	366.74			

Dr		I Harris Account			Cr
Date	Details	£	Date	Details	£
18/08/14	SDB 15	385.87	31/08/14	Balance c/d	385.87
		385.87			385.87
01/09/14	Balance b/d	385.87			

Dr		J Clarke Account			Cr
Date	Details	£	Date	Details	£
26/08/14	SDB 15	311.82	31/08/14	Balance c/d	311.82
		311.82			311.82
01/09/14	Balance b/d	311.82			

Dr		K Khan Account			Cr
Date	Details	£	Date	Details	£
27/08/14	SDB 15	395.70	31/08/14	Balance c/d	395.70
		395.70			395.70
01/09/14	Balance b/d	395.70			

(It is quite common for accounts with only one entry to be left as they are and not balanced since the one figure will be carried forward to the next period).

MAIN LEDGER

Dr		Sales Account (Clothes)			Cr
Date	Details	£	Date	Details	£
31/08/14	Balance c/d	1106.32	31/08/14	SDB 15	1106.32
		1106.32			1106.32
			01/09/14	Balance b/d	1106.32

Dr		Sales Returns Account (Clothes)			Cr
Date	Details	£	Date	Details	£
31/08/14	SRDB 02	160.00	31/08/14	Balance c/d	160.00
		160.00			160.00
01/09/14	Balance b/d	160.00			

Dr		Sales Account (Fabrics)			Cr
Date	Details	£	Date	Details	£
31/08/14	Balance c/d	581.41	31/08/14	SDB 15	581.41
		581.41			581.41
			01/09/14	Balance b/d	581.41

Dr		Sales Returns Account (Fabrics)			Cr
Date	Details	£	Date	Details	£

Dr		VAT Account			Cr
Date	Details	£	Date	Details	£
31/08/14	SRDB 02	32.00	31/08/14	SDB 15	337.54
31/08/14	Balance c/d	305.54			
		337.54			337.54
			01/09/14	Balance b/d	305.54

Dr		Sales Ledger Control Account			Cr
Date	Details	£	Date	Details	£
31/08/14	SDB 15	2025.27	31/08/14	SRDB 02	192.00
			31/08/14	Balance c/d	1833.27
		2025.27			2025.27
01/09/14	Balance b/d	1833.27			

Follow through the stages for balancing each account and ensure you understand how each account has been balanced. You should note that each account will now **only** have either a debit balance or a credit balance. Accounts do not have a mixture of debit and credit balances.

If you now add up all the debit **balances** in the main ledger and compare them with the credit **balances** they will still come to the same figure as each other.

Let us now do another reconciliation of the Sales Ledger Control.

Reconciliation of Sales Ledger Control Account 31st August 2014		
	£	**£**
G Hall	373.14	
H Lewis	366.74	
I Harris	385.87	
J Clarke	311.82	
K Khan	395.70	
TOTAL	**1833.27**	
TOTAL PER SALES LEDGER CONTROL		**1833.27**
Discrepancy (if any)	nil	

You should note that we only need to use the balances on each account, but even so the sum of the individual customer accounts should still arrive at the same figure as on the Sales Ledger Control Account.

Aged Debtor Analysis

A variation on a Sales Ledger is the Aged Debtor Report. This can be drawn up manually or using a computer accounting package. While it is important to know who owes you money and how much, it is even more important to know when it was owed. If we have offered our customers credit terms we need to know that they have paid, and if they haven't paid how overdue it is. An example is given below:

Aged Debtors						
Account	**Credit Limit**	**Balance £**	**Up to 30 days £**	**31 – 60 days £**	**61 – 90 Days £**	**91 days and over £**
G Hall	1000	275.00	275.00	0.00	0.00	0.00
H Lewis	750	650.00	425.00	225.00	0.00	0.00
I Harris	2000	1050.00	750.00	200.00	100.00	0.00
J Clarke	1500	750.00	750.00	0.00	0.00	0.00
K Khan	750	300.00	0.00	0.00	0.00	300.00

Here each customer is listed with their credit limit. The credit limit is how much we have decided they can buy at any one time. A customer should not be able to buy goods worth more than the credit limit until they have paid off at least some of the amount owing.

In this case the terms are on 30 days since the 1st analysis column says 'Up to 30 days'. This means that the invoices which come to this amount are still within the terms of business.

The next analysis column says '31 – 60 days'. The amounts in this column are overdue. The invoices are 31 to 60 days old meaning they are 1 to 30 days overdue. (Remember you have allowed them 30 days to pay so they do not become overdue until they are 31 days old). The invoices in this column need chasing. How this is done will be determined by the company policy but usually a telephone call or a letter is sent by way of a reminder.

The next column is '61 – 90 days'. The invoices included in this column are seriously overdue. They are between 31 and 60 days overdue. Your company will probably be sending a letter threatening legal action and the customer will be put on stop. Putting a customer on stop means that you will not supply them with any more goods until the overdue invoice(s) have been settled.

The final column is '91 days and over'. This means that the invoice(s) will be overdue by more than 60 days. Your company will probably contact a debt collection agency to recover the debt and they will probably start legal action.

What steps to take to recover the overdue accounts is up to the company itself, but larger company will probably have a credit control department whose job it is to monitor and attempt to recover overdue amounts.

Chapter Summary

Invoices are first recorded in the Sales Day Book.

The amounts in the Sales Day Book are entered into the Sales Ledger accounts and the Main Ledger accounts. The Sales Ledger accounts should be debited and the Sales account should be credited.

VAT is not included in the Sales account but recorded in its own account. Entries in the customer accounts **do** include VAT.

The total of the debits must always equal the total of the credits.

'Control' accounts are summary accounts, used to summarise a group or ledger.

If a Sales Ledger Control account is used, the individual customer accounts become part of the Subsidiary Sales Ledger and will not be part of the double entry.

The Sales Ledger Control account is reconciled to the individual customer accounts at regular intervals.

Credit Notes are recorded in the Sales Returns Day Book and then **credited** to the individual customer accounts. The Sales Returns account will be debited.

The net amount only is recorded in the Sales account or the Sales Returns account. The gross amount is recorded in the individual customer accounts and the Sales Ledger Control account.

Accounts are balanced at regular intervals. Only the balance on the account should be used to reconcile the Sales Ledger Control account.

Accounts have either a debit balance or a credit balance, but not both.

CHAPTER 4
Recording Sales and Sales Returns

Practice Questions

Chapter 4

4.1 Enter the following credit sales in the Sales day Book. (VAT is charged at 20%). Total the Sales Day Book for the week.

2015

Jan 5th	Goods sold to M Harvey	£50 plus VAT	Invoice 23579
Jan 5th	Goods sold to N Pearson	£76 plus VAT	Invoice 23580
Jan 6th	Goods sold to P Murray	£112 plus VAT	Invoice 23581
Jan 7th	Goods sold to M Harvey	£75 plus VAT	Invoice 23582
Jan 7th	Goods sold to R Graham	£99 plus VAT	Invoice 23583
Jan 8th	Goods sold to P Murray	£45 plus VAT	Invoice 23584
Jan 9th	Goods sold to S Walsh	£80 plus VAT	Invoice 23585
Jan 9th	Goods sold to M Harvey	£55 plus VAT	Invoice 23586

M Harvey account is SL 23
P Murray account is SL 45
S Walsh account is SL 79
N Pearson account is SL 52
R Graham account is SL 15

SALES DAY BOOK **SDB 101**

Date	Invoice	Customer	Folio	Total		Sales		VAT	
				£	p	£	p	£	p
		TOTAL FOR THE WEEK							

4.2 Using the answers for task 4.1 post the Sales Day Book to the Main Ledger accounts and the individual customer accounts. The accounts are shown on p72 and 73.

4.3 The following Credit Notes were issued in the same week. Enter these in the Sales Returns Day Book.

2015			
6th Jan	Issued Credit Note to M Harvey	£24.00 including VAT	CN239
8th Jan	Issued Credit Note to P Murray	£20.40 including VAT	CN240

SALES RETURNS DAY BOOK **SRDB 12**

Date	Cr Note	Customer	Folio	Total		Sales Clothes		VAT	
				£	p	£	p	£	p
		TOTAL FOR THE WEEK							

4.4 Using the answers for task 4.3 post the Sales Returns Day Book to the Main Ledger accounts and the individual customer accounts. Use the accounts already prepared in task 4.2.

4.5 Balance all the accounts.

4.6 Reconcile the Sales Ledger Control account to the Sales Ledger accounts.

SALES LEDGER

Dr	R Graham Account (SL 15)				Cr
Date	Details	£	Date	Details	£

Dr	M Harvey Account (SL 23)				Cr
Date	Details	£	Date	Details	£

Dr	P Murray Account (SL 45)				Cr
Date	Details	£	Date	Details	£

Dr	N Pearson Account (SL 52)				Cr
Date	Details	£	Date	Details	£

Dr	S Walsh Account (SL 79)				Cr
Date	Details	£	Date	Details	£

CHAPTER 4
Recording Sales and Sales Returns

MAIN LEDGER

Dr		Sales Account (4000)			Cr
Date	Details	£	Date	Details	£

Dr		Sales Returns Account (4050)			Cr
Date	Details	£	Date	Details	£

Dr		VAT Account (2200)			Cr
Date	Details	£	Date	Details	£

Dr		Sales Ledger Control Account (1100)			Cr
Date	Details	£	Date	Details	£

Reconciliation of Sales Ledger Control Account
9th January 2015

	£	£
R Graham		
M Harvey		
P Murray		
N Pearson		
S Walsh		
TOTAL		
TOTAL PER SALES LEDGER CONTROL		
Discrepancy (if any)		

Chapter 5

Cash Receipts and Cash Sales

> In this chapter we will be looking at how we record a cash receipt in our books.
>
> We will look at what 'cash' is in accounting terms
>
> We shall see how to record cash sales
>
> We shall become familiar with the cash book (receipts side)
>
> We shall look at the various methods of payment

So far in this book we have seen how to record credit sales. A big part of many businesses is the cash sales.

Cash sales

In accounting terms, '**cash**' means anything that isn't on credit. So a cash payment will include coins and bank notes, cheques, debit card payments, credit card payments, and electronic transfer payments. We will look at each method of payment in detail later in this chapter.

When cash is received by a business it must be recorded at once. In most retail businesses this is done by means of a **cash till**. These vary in complexity. The simplest ones have a till roll which will give a total of all receipts during the day. This can then be checked with the amounts actually in the till at the end of the day. The more complex ones store the sales totals electronically and will even update stock levels as each sale is made.

If you receive cheques and other money by post you may have a **remittance list**. Remittance simply means what money you have been sent in payment for goods or services. The remittance list is a list of cheques and money received. You would record the date, the sender and the amount. This would then be totalled at regular periods (day or week) ready for payment into the bank.

If you don't have a till, then you may combine the remittance list with a cash received list. This is the same as the remittance list described above, but will also include any cash payments made to you.

Whatever method you use, it will eventually be recorded in the **cash book**. A cash book is used to record all the monetary transactions of a business. Typically a cash book will have a column for bank transactions and one for cash transactions. Transactions are 'cash' until they are actually banked, so it is quite possible to have cheque amounts in the 'cash' column. It will depend on how the cash book is used (for each transaction or if there is just a total at the end of the day ready for payment into the bank).

CASH BOOK

RECEIPTS | PAYMENTS

Date	Detail	Cash £	Bank £	Date	Detail	Cash £	Bank £

(It is quite acceptable to use separate cash and bank accounts, but using a cash book is the more normal practice.)

Points to note about the cash book

> You will notice that the cash book follows the same principles as any other 'T' account. The debits (on the left) are for 'receiving' and the credits (on the right) are for 'giving'.
>
> The cash book usually doubles as a book of prime entry **and** part of the double entry system. Therefore, any entry in the cash book will need a balancing entry in some other account.
>
> The cash book will look different in different companies. Some companies which bank all of their cash daily may not have a cash column. It is not necessary for them to know how much cash is left on the premises. (Small amounts of cash for sundry items such as tea, coffee, stamps, window cleaning etc are recorded in the Petty Cash Book which we will look at later in this book).
>
> Some companies will need to analyse their receipts and (particularly) their payments so that a check can be kept on what the amounts in the cash book are for. (We will look at this later in this chapter).

Let us now see how we can record a cash sale in our books.

Let us suppose that a customer comes into our shop and buys goods for £300.00 plus VAT in cash.

CASH BOOK

RECEIPTS | CB125 PAYMENTS

Date	Detail	Cash £		Bank £		Date	Detail	Cash £		Bank £	
25/08	Cash Sale	360	00								

Dr		Sales Account			Cr
Date	Details	£	Date	Details	£
			25/08/13	CB125	300.00

Dr		VAT Account			Cr
Date	Details	£	Date	Details	£
			25/08/13	CB125	60.00

This is the same as recording a credit sale except that we are using the cash book instead of the Sales Ledger or the Sales Ledger Control. Remember that the Sales Ledger records show us how much each customer owes us, but if they pay by cash then they don't owe us anything. We have the money in cash ready for banking.

You should notice that the total of the debits still equals the total of the credits (£360.00 = £300.00 + £60.00).

Other cash receipts

Not all cash receipts will be for sales. In Chapter 4 we saw how we recorded credit sales. The amount each customer owes us is shown in the individual customer account. So there will come a time when our credit customer will actually pay us for the goods.

Refer to the account of G Hall on p64.

CHAPTER 5

Cash Receipts and Cash Sales

Suppose that G Hall pays his invoice by post with a cheque and it arrives on 2nd September. The entries for this will **not** include an entry for VAT or for a sale. The sale was made and recorded by the invoice on 4th August and the credit note was issued on the 6th. This means that G Hall owes £373.14 which is the amount he pays by cheque. The entries required for the receipt of this cheque are as follows:

CASH BOOK

RECEIPTS | CB125 PAYMENTS

Date	Detail	Cash £		Bank £		Date	Detail	Cash £		Bank £	
25/08	Cash Sale	360	00								
02/09	**G Hall**			**373**	**14**						

Dr		**Sales Ledger Control Account**			Cr
Date	Details	£	Date	Details	£
31/08/13	SDB 15	2025.27	31/08/13	SRDB 02	192.00
			02/09/13	**CB125**	**373.14**

Don't forget that you will also need to update the Subsidiary Sales Ledger

Dr		**G Hall Account**			Cr
Date	Details	£	Date	Details	£
04/08/13	SDB 15	421.14	06/08/13	SRDB 02	48.00
			02/09/13	**CB125**	**373.14**

Points to note are:

The amount is shown in the Bank column as it is a cheque and will be banked immediately.

Not all the accounts have been shown here, but if they were then the debits would still equal the credits for the main ledger accounts.

Not all the customer accounts are shown here, but if they were the total of all the customer account balances would equal the balance on the Sales Ledger Control.

The principle of 'giving' being a credit entry is now becoming a little obscure. In the Sales Ledger and the Sales Ledger Control it may be easier to think of debit entries increasing what the customer owes and credit entries reducing the amount.

LEARNING POINT

Many students make the error of recording sales and VAT when payment is made by a credit customer. Make sure you know whether the receipt of cash is for a cash sale or a payment from a credit customer. Make sure you know how to deal with both kinds of receipt.

Recording the payments to the bank

There will come a time when we will pay the cash (as shown in the cash book) into the bank. We will need to reflect this in our cash book. This is done by means of a **contra**. The word 'contra' means 'opposite' or 'against'. In accounting terms it is when one account is set off against an opposite entry in another. If we pay the cash into the bank we will increase the amount in the bank and decrease the amount of cash. The contra entry will be identified by a 'c'.

CASH BOOK

RECEIPTS | CB125 PAYMENTS

Date	Detail	Cash £		Bank £		Date	Detail	Cash £		Bank £	
25/08	Cash Sale	360	00			**02/09**	**Bank (c)**	**360**	**00**		
02/09	G Hall			373	14						
02/09	**Cash (c)**			**360**	**00**						

Notice the entries. The cash column has been credited with the cash as this has been 'given' to the bank and the bank column has been debited as the amount has been 'received' by the bank. The details column shows where the other side of the double entry is and is further explained by the (c) meaning contra entry.

CHAPTER 5

Cash Receipts and Cash Sales

The three column cash book

A slightly more advanced for of cash book is the **three column** cash book. It is called three columns because there are three columns for figures on each side. In addition to the cash and bank columns of the two column cash book, there is now an additional column for discounts. These discounts will be settlement (or cash) discounts. (Other kinds of discounts are not shown in the accounts.) An example is given below.

CASHBOOK CBR25

Date	Detail	Discount Allowed	Cash	Bank	Date	Detail	Discount Received	Cash	Bank
		£	£	£			£	£	£
01/09/14	Balance b/d		360.52	150.75	01/09/14	Cash Purchase		300.00	
01/09/14	Cash Sales		480.00		08/09/14	M Ahmed	10.00		290.00
08/09/14	G Hall	15.00		223.25	15/09/14	Rent			95.25
15/09/14	K Khan			350.00	22/09/14	C Kaur			534.96
22/09/14	Cash Sales		600.00		27/09/14	Wages			525.50
27/09/14	Cash Sales		120.00		27/09/14	Cash Purchase		360.00	
29/09/14	Cash (c)			500.00	29/09/14	Bank (c)		500.00	

Let us look at each of the entries starting with the debit entries.

01/09/14 Balance b/d is the amount of cash in hand and money at the bank at the end of the previous month. (We will see how to balance the cash book later).

01/09/14 Cash Sales – this is the record of the cash sales. The total amount of cash paid by the customer is entered in the cash column. This may not be just one customer but it could be the total in the till at the end of the day or period. Remember it may be notes and coins or it may be cheques (which we have not yet banked) or it may be a mixture of both.

08/09/14 G Hall – this is the credit customer G Hall paying his invoice. He has been allowed (and he has taken) a discount of £10.00 for prompt payment as would have been offered on the invoice. Remember that only settlement discounts need to be recorded in the accounts because it is not clear at the time of raising the invoice whether the discount will be taken or not. Trade and Bulk discounts are given as a matter of course. The total invoice amount would have been £233.25 but due to the settlement discount the cheque received will only be for £223.25. The payment would probably have been by direct debit or some means of electronic transfer as the amount is showing directly in the bank account.

15/09/14 K Khan – this is the credit customer K Khan paying his invoice. There is no settlement discount, either because K Khan has paid too late to take advantage of it, or because he was not offered one in the first place. Again, the payment would probably have been by direct debit or some means of electronic transfer as the amount is showing directly in the bank account.

The entries for 22/09/14 and 27/09/14 are more cash sales. The totals are recorded in the cash column. Remember that this could be cash AND cheques as cheques are still considered to be 'cash' until they are banked.

We will leave the final entry for a moment and look at the credit side.

01/09/14. This is a cash purchase. Money would have been taken from the till or safe to pay for the goods.

08/09/14 M Ahmed – this is a payment to one of our credit suppliers. It could be a cheque payment but more likely an electronic payment since there is no cheque number stated. The invoice would have been for £300 but we are paying £290 and taking £10 settlement discount.

15/09/14. This is a payment of rent. It will probably be a standing order or a direct debit payment as there is again no cheque number.

22/09/14 C Kaur – this is a payment to another of our credit suppliers. It could be a cheque payment but more likely an electronic payment since there is no cheque number stated. There is no settlement discount, either because we have paid too late to take advantage of it, or because we were not offered one in the first place.

27/09/14 Wages – this is the payment of wages to our staff. It is most likely a BACS payment. It isn't a cheque as there is no cheque number.

27/09/14. This is another cash purchase. Money would have been taken from the till or safe to pay for the goods.

Now let us return to the final entry on the debit side.

This is telling us that £500 cash has been put into the bank. The entry is in the bank column showing money going into the bank with the details as 'cash'. The (c) tells us it is a contra entry (see p79). The corresponding entry is on the credit side of the cash book in the cash column showing money going from cash with the details as 'bank'.

Balancing the cash book

We will now see how you should balance the cash book.

CASHBOOK CBR25

Date	Detail	Discount Allowed	Cash	Bank	Date	Detail	Discount Received	Cash	Bank
		£	£	£			£	£	£
01/09/14	Balance b/d		360.52	150.75	01/09/14	Cash Purchase		300.00	
01/09/14	Cash Sales		480.00		08/09/14	M Ahmed	10.00		290.00
08/09/14	G Hall	15.00		223.25	15/09/14	Rent			95.25
15/09/14	K Khan			350.00	22/09/14	C Kaur			534.96
22/09/14	Cash Sales		600.00		27/09/14	Wages			525.50
27/09/14	Cash Sales		120.00		27/09/14	Cash Purchase		360.00	
29/09/14	Cash (c)			500.00	29/09/14	Bank (c)		500.00	
30/09/14	**Balance c/d**			**221.71**	**30/09/14**	**Balance c/d**		**400.52**	
		15.00	**1560.52**	**1445.71**			**10.00**	**1560.52**	**1445.71**
01/10/14	**Balance c/d**		**400.52**		**01/10/14**	**Balance c/d**			**221.71**

The entries in bold are those required when balancing the cash book. Let us look at the process. We will deal with the cash columns first.

In the cash column the total of the debit entries (money coming into the business) plus the opening balance **must** be more than the credit entries (money going out of the business). You cannot spend more cash that you have actually have. Therefore you should add up all the debit entries in the cash column and put the total at the bottom suitably ruled off. In this case the total is £1560.52.

This figure **must** now go at the bottom of the cash column on the credit side of the cash book. £1560.52 is the balancing figure.

We now have to find the missing figure. This will be the figure which, when added to the total of the other cash column entries, makes the total £1560.52. One way of establishing this figure is to subtract all the entries from the balancing figure. (£1560.52 - £300.00 - £360.00 - £500.00 = £400.52). You should create a new row for this figure calling it Balance c/d (carried down).

This balance amount should then be transferred to the **debit** side of the cash book as a balance b/d (brought down). You must make sure that the balance b/d is entered **below** the total figures. Note that the date for the balance b/d is the day after the balance c/d. Although this may not be followed in actual fact, the principle is that the balance c/d is at the close of business one day and the balance b/d is at the start of business the next day.

Now let us look at the bank columns. We need to establish which side (debits or credits) has the greater total. We cannot be sure which it should be since it **is** possible to take more money from the bank than we put in when we have an overdraft facility. If we total the debits and then the credits we will see that in this case the credit side has the greater total (£1445.71). More money has been taken from the bank than we have in. This means that there is an overdraft.

Following the same principle as for the cash columns, this balancing figure should be put at the bottom of both the bank columns. The missing figure from the debit side must now be calculated. (£1445.71 - £150.75 - £223.25 - £350.00 - £500.00 = £221.71). The new row created for the cash column balance c/d should now be used for the bank balance c/d.

This balance amount should then be transferred to the **credit** side of the cash book as a balance b/d (brought down). You must make sure that the balance b/d is entered **below** the total figures. The credit balance b/d means that the company is £221.71 overdrawn.

Finally we should total the discount allowed column and the discount received column and put the figures in the row we have used for the total figures. There are no balances to b/d or c/d as the discounts are shown purely as a memorandum. As we shall see in a moment, the discounts will be shown in the main ledger completely separately from the bank and cash balances.

Analysed cash book

You may have realised that there will be numerous entries in the cash book. Since it is a book of prime entry, all cash and bank transactions will be shown here and it may only be updated to the rest of the main ledger daily, weekly or even monthly. By the time we update the rest of the main ledger there may be tens of entries and sorting out the cash sales from the payments by credit customers can be time consuming and could lead to errors. For this reason many businesses keep a cash book with analysis columns.

On the next page we will just look at the receipts side of an analysed cash book. We will use the figures shown in the three column cash book.

CASHBOOK - RECEIPTS CBR25

Date	Detail	Folio	Discount Allowed		Cash		Bank		Cash Sales		VAT		Sales Ledger		Sundry	
			£	p	£	p	£	p	£	p	£	p	£	p	£	p
01/09/14	Balance b/d				360	52	150	75								
01/09/14	Cash Sales	ML			480	00			400	00	80	00				
08/09/14	G Hall	SL	10	00			223	25					223	25		
15/09/14	K Khan	SL					350	00					350	00		
22/09/14	Cash Sales	ML			600	00			500	00	100	00				
29/09/14	Cash Sales	ML			120	00			100	00	20	00				
29/09/14	Cash (c)	-					500	00								
30/09/14	**Balance c/d**						221	71								
			10	**00**	**1560**	**52**	**1445**	**71**	**1000**	**00**	**200**	**00**	**573**	**25**	**0**	**00**

Let us look at each line of the analysed cash book in turn.

01/09/14 Balance b/d is the amount of cash and money at the bank at the end of the previous month.

01/09/14 Cash Sales – this is the record the cash sales. The total amount of cash paid by the customers is entered in the cash column, while the net amount is shown in the cash sales column and the VAT amount is shown in the VAT column. The folio column shows Main Ledger entries (ML) and Sales Ledger entries (SL).

08/09/14 G Hall – this is the credit customer G Hall paying his invoice. Remember the total invoice amount would have been £233.25 but due to the settlement discount the cheque received will only be for £223.25. Note how the amount actually paid is shown in the Sales Ledger column.

15/09/14 K Khan – this is the credit customer K Khan paying his invoice. Again the amount actually paid is shown in the Sales Ledger column.

The entries for 22/09/14 and 29/09/14 are more cash sales. The totals are recorded in the cash column. The net amount is recorded in the cash sales column and the VAT amount in the VAT column.

If the cash book is used as part of the main ledger the contra will not need to be shown anywhere else in the accounts. If it isn't part of the main ledger there will be an entry in the debit entry in the bank account and a credit entry in the cash account.

We can only see the balance c/d because you will remember we are showing only the debit side of the analysed cash book.

LEARNING POINT

Just because there are lots of boxes to enter amounts in the analysed cash book does not mean that you have to fill them all. Remember that the analysis column is there to analyse the receipt; it is impossible for a receipt to cover all the points of analysis. For example a receipt from a credit customer cannot also be a cash sale so you **must** leave this column blank.

The one column which has nothing in is the Sundry column. Entries in this column would include such items as:

Rental income from letting out spare office space
Income from a loan
Money introduced from the owner's private funds (known as 'capital')

You will see that the columns are totalled at regular intervals (in this case, monthly).

The cash column total is the total of all cash received in the month plus the opening balance. It may not be the cash in hand you have as we have only dealt with the cash receipts. ('Cash in hand' means the notes and coins you have on the premises). Cash payments will be shown on the other side of the cash book.

The bank column similarly will show all the amounts paid into the bank in the month plus the opening balance. Again this may not be the amount you have in the bank as we have only dealt with the bank receipts. Bank payments will have been made and shown on the other side of the cash book (the payments or credit side).

Checking your cash book

When you have an analysed cash book you can check the accuracy of your totals. The sum of the cash and bank columns less the opening balances should equal the sum of the other totals (but not the discounts allowed).

The cash column less the opening balance = £1560.52 - £360.52 = £1200.00
The bank column less the opening balance = £1524.00 - £950.75 = £573.25

Total of the two columns less the opening balances = £1200.00 + £573.25 = **£1773.25**.

The totals of the other columns are:

Cash Sales = £1000.00

VAT = £200.00

Sales Ledger = £573.25

Total = £1000.00 + £200.00 + £573.25 = **£1773.25**

The discounts allowed column is not included in this total as it is a memorandum column only. Whereas half of the double entry has been recorded in the cash book already for cash sales, VAT and Sales Ledger Control, the discounts allowed is recorded here purely as a prime entry.

The double entry required for the other side of the cash book entries is as follows:

Dr			**Sales Account**		Cr
Date	Details	£	Date	Details	£
			30/09/14	CBR25	1000.00

Dr	**VAT Account**				Cr
Date	Details	£	Date	Details	£
			30/09/14	CBR25	200.00

Dr	**Sales Ledger Control Account**				Cr
Date	Details	£	Date	Details	£
			30/09/14	CBR25	573.25
			30/09/14	Disc Allowed	10.00

Dr	**Discounts Allowed Account**				Cr
Date	Details	£	Date	Details	£
30/09/14	CBR25	10.00			

You must not forget to update the Sales Ledger. The customer accounts must be updated with the amount they have paid **and the discount allowed**. Each transaction will be shown separately in the individual customer account. You may need to refer to the customer account in case of query and so you will need to see each individual transaction.

Dr	**G Hall Account**				Cr
Date	Details	£	Date	Details	£
			08/09/14	CBR25	223.25
			08/09/14	Disc Allowed	10.00

Dr	**K Khan Account**				Cr
Date	Details	£	Date	Details	£
			15/09/14	CBR25	350.00

You will have noticed that we have introduced a **discounts allowed account** in the main ledger. This is because the discount is not a cash transaction and as such is not shown in the cash or bank columns of the cash book (unlike the cash sales and the receipts from the credit customers). Strictly speaking it is not a cash book entry at all, but it is shown in the cash book as a means of showing why the receipt from the customer was not the total amount of the invoice. Since it is not shown in the cash or bank columns of the cash book, it needs its own double entry.

LEARNING POINT

Students often make errors by trying to put the total amount of the invoice somewhere in the cash book, the Sales Ledger or the Sales Ledger Control. While this is fine when a customer is paying the invoice in full, when settlement discounts are offered you must remember that we are recording the cash transaction. The amount of the cash receipt is the important entry as the amount of the invoice has been recorded elsewhere and at a previous time.

You should remember to record the amount paid by the customer and then record any discount afterwards.

You should also remember that customers will not pay the total amount of the invoice if they are entitled to a discount. Therefore you must be aware that the cheque paid by the customer may not be the amount on the invoice.

Remittance advice

Receipts from credit customers must be checked to ensure what the cheque is actually for. Remind yourself of the customer account for Morris & Sons on p62. Suppose we receive a cheque from them for £1665.00. What exactly is this payment for? It could be for anything. Some companies will pay an amount on account, meaning that they will pay a certain amount each week or month. This is a little unsatisfactory as we cannot link the payment with the invoices supplied. We can never be sure if an invoice has been missed or a discount taken when it is not available.

The solution to this problem is a **remittance advice**. A remittance advice is a document which usually accompanies the cheque saying what the payment is for. Typically it will show the invoices to be paid and the credit notes and discounts taken. Some companies provide a tear-off slip with their statement of account.

LEARNING POINT

You will notice how the figures in brackets are amounts to be taken **off** the total of the invoices to be paid. Putting figures in brackets is a common (and acceptable) way of showing negative amounts.

MORRIS & SONS

45 Scartho Street, Immingham, IM15 2BH

Remittance advice

Supplier:

Date	Transaction ref	Amount (£)
30/07/2014	Invoice 36598	490.00
01/08/2014	Invoice 36701	500.00
04/08/2014	Credit Note CN 365	(90.00)
08/08/2014	Invoice 36852	360.00
11/08/2014	Credit Note CN 370	(30.00)
15/08/2014	Invoice 36921	490.00
15/08/2014	Discount on Inv 36921	(10.00)
18/08/2014	Credit Note 375	(45.00)

CHEQUE TOTAL	**£1665.00**

Now we have this remittance advice it becomes quite clear what is being paid for. It is also a document which is important to both companies. The copy of this remittance advice is useful to Morris & Sons as it shows that a payment was made to cover these transactions. To our company it shows which invoices have been paid and by implication, which invoices are still outstanding.

BACS

Another method of payment which you may receive is a **BACS transfer**. BACS stands for Bankers Automated Clearing Service. BACS is the company which organises Standing Orders and Direct Debits.

A BACS payment can be set up by individuals who make regular payments. BACS is the company that sets the rules for **standing order**, a **direct debit** or a **direct credit.**

> A standing order is an instruction a bank account holder gives to their bank to pay a set amount at regular intervals to another account. The instructions to pay come from the person sending the money.
>
> A direct debit is the same as a standing order except that the instructions to pay come from the person receiving the money.
>
> A direct credit is mainly used for paying wages and salaries, but is also used by many companies to pay suppliers.

BACS started in 1968. While it is much quicker and cheaper than cheques, it has come under much criticism as it still takes 3 days for BACS payments to clear. There is an alternative to BACS known as **CHAPS (**Clearing House Automated Payment System). CHAPS offers same day transfers, but it can be expensive (typically £30 per transaction). It is therefore used mainly for large transfers of money.

The government commissioned a company called VocaLink to set up another system which would be much quicker and cheaper. On 27th May 2008 the first transaction using **FPS** (Faster Payments Service) was processed, which transfers money between bank accounts almost instantaneously. At the moment it will run alongside BACS, but hopes are that it will replace BACS altogether.

The problem with an automated payment is that the receiving company doesn't know when, or even if at all, a payment has been made. It will show on the bank statement for the end of the month, but if the transfer is made at the beginning of the month it could be over a month before the seller knows that a payment has been made. The problem is solved by the buyer sending a BACS (or FPS) remittance advice. There are many styles of BACS remittance advice, but they usually contain the same information as the example above.

EFTPOS (Electronic Funds Transfer at Point Of Sale)

EFTPOS is the method used for accepting **debit cards** and **credit cards**. On making a purchase, the customer inserts a debit card or credit card into an on-site machine. When the customer confirms the purchase by security PIN (Personal Identification Number), the equipment contacts the store's bank electronically about the transaction. A message is also sent to the customer's bank. Unless there is reason for the transaction not to be completed, the funds will then be transferred between the two accounts. The transaction only takes a few seconds. The cards now issued are called Chip and PIN. The chip is the embedded integrated circuit which processes the information. It is the gold coloured square which can be seen on the face of the card.

The difference between a debit card and a credit card is that the debit card is linked directly to the customer's bank account. Amounts will be taken straight from the customer's account. A credit card payment will be notified to the customer's bank and a statement will be sent to the customer monthly. The customer can then choose to pay off the total amount, or to pay part of the bill. If only part of the bill is paid then interest will be charged on the balance.

If you need to take payment from a customer with a debit or credit card you will need to make sure that:

The card has a logo and a chip
The card is in date (i.e. that today's date is between the 'valid from' date and the 'expires on' date)
The card has not been tampered with and there is a signature on the reverse.

The old style of chip and signature (or the even older magnetic strip and signature) can no longer be a guarantee for payment. There are three exceptions to this:

Customers with the old style card which has not yet been upgraded
Some disabled cardholders
Cardholders from countries which have not yet upgraded to chip and PIN.

Prepayment cards

Prepayment cards can be used like credit or debit cards but before they can be used you have to 'load' money onto them. Some prepayment cards are used only once, while others can be topped up at a bank, Post Office or PayPoint terminal (depending on the card used). They can even be topped up online or over the phone.

Prepayment cards are ideal for people who can't get, or don't want, a credit card. They are more secure to use online than a credit card or debit card because they are not linked to a particular bank account, but charges are often made for the card in the first place and to top up the card.

Prepayment cards can also be loaded with foreign currency so they can be used while travelling abroad.

Some prepayment cards can only be used for predefined items. These are known as closed system prepayment cards. An Oyster Card on the London transport system is an example of a closed system prepayment card.

Floor limit

A floor limit is the payment amount above which credit or debit card transactions must be authorised before being processed. The floor limit can vary from business to business and is set by the card company. It has to a certain extent become unnecessary, as authorisation of debit or credit cards is done electronically. However, it may occasionally still be used if the customer doesn't have a chip and PIN card or if there is a problem in the connection to the card company's electronic authorisation system. If the transaction is below the floor limit then no authorisation is required. If it's above the floor limit then you must contact the card company (probably by telephone) or the payment cannot be guaranteed. (It is worth noting that the floor limit for all telephone, mail order or internet transactions is zero).

Cheques

A cheque is a written instruction to a bank (the drawee) to pay a specific amount to another person (the payee). It is written by the bank's customer (the drawer).

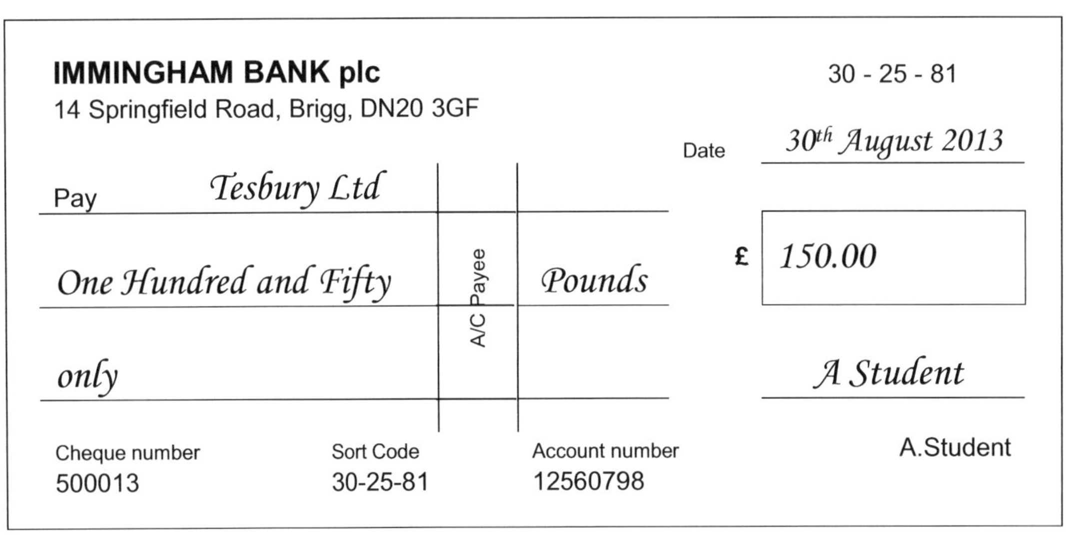

In the example of a cheque on the previous page:

The drawee is Immingham Bank plc
The drawer is A Student
The payee is Tesbury Ltd

When you receive a cheque you must check the following points:

1. That it is signed
2. That the date is today's date or earlier, but not earlier than 6 months. (Cheques are no longer valid after 6 months)
3. The words and figures agree
4. The payee's name is correct.

If it is not signed or any of the other items are incorrect or missing then the cheque will not be paid by the bank and returned to the payee.

A **banker's draft** is almost identical to a cheque except that the drawer and the drawee are one and the same. A customer can order a banker's draft from the bank, usually for large purchases. The bank will take the funds from the customer before it issues the draft. The advantage is that the funds for payment are from the bank itself rather than the customer's account. In this way it is more secure than a cheque.

Postal Orders are essentially cheques for people without bank accounts. They can be purchased from the Post Office and used as payment for goods and services. They are particularly useful when paying by post if a cheque is not possible. If you receive one, it should be paid into a bank account in the same way as cheques.

Crossings

You will have noticed the two vertical lines on the above cheque with the words 'a/c payee' written in between. This means that the cheque can only be paid into the payee's bank account. This is a security measure so that a lost cheque is virtually useless to someone who finds it. To find a cheque issued by a bank without this crossing is very rare nowadays. Had it not had this crossing then it would be fully transferable, meaning that it could be passed to someone else if it was signed on the back (endorsed). A crossing without words means that the cheque has to be paid into a bank account (i.e. it cannot be exchanged for cash at the bank). Another possibility is to write the actual branch of the bank it is to be paid into between these lines.

Cheque guarantee cards

Cheques may be issued to customers with a cheque guarantee card (often this is the same card as the debit card as described above). This is useful to the payee as it guarantees payment of the cheque up to a certain limit set by the bank, whether or not the customer has enough funds in his/her account to cover it. When receiving a cheque with a cheque guarantee card you will need to write the card number on the back of the cheque.

The guarantee is per transaction, so you cannot overcome the limit by writing two or more cheques for the same payment.

Cash

Finally we come to payment by cash (here meaning coins and bank notes). Bank notes and coins must be accepted as payment from whoever bears them. This is both an advantage and a disadvantage. It is an advantage as there can be no dispute over payment. The coins and notes are legal tender and cannot be disputed. The disadvantage is that they belong to whoever bears them, so theft is a real threat.

> Bank notes can be used for any amount as can £1 and £2 coins.
> 50p and 20p coins are only legal tender up to £10.
> 10p and 5p coins are legal tender up to £5
> 2p and 1p coins are legal tender up to 20p

If you receive more than this in coins you are entitled to refuse them (though customer relations may suffer if you do!).

Payment by coins and notes should be for the exact amount as legally you cannot demand change. However, the vast majority of suppliers (if not all suppliers) will give change.

In order to give change, shops and businesses which deal in cash transactions will keep a **float** in their till. A float is a selection of coins and notes which will be kept in the till at the start of the day so that early customers can be given change. How much the float will be will depend on the company and the amount of cash usually needed.

LEARNING POINT

When you check the contents of your till at the end of the day, you must be sure to take off the till float to arrive at the takings for the day.

If you are comparing the contents of the till with the till roll, then you must remember to add on the till float you had at the beginning of the day.

When taking payments by cash you must be aware of the security problems:

> Cash should be kept in the till and the till should be closed except when actually being used.

If you don't keep a till then money should be kept in cash box or safe which is locked. The keys to the box or safe should be limited and kept away from the box or safe.

Cash should be banked as soon as possible.

The contents of the till should be checked with the till roll at least every day, preferably by someone else other than the person taking the cash payments.

Chapter Summary

'Cash' in accounting terms means cheques and card payments as well as notes and coins.

Cash transactions are recorded in a cash book.

Cash received can be for sales or payment against previous invoices. Other receipts are possible but less regular or common.

Each kind of cash receipt will be recorded differently in the accounts and in the analysed cash book.

Discounts are not strictly speaking a cash book entry, but they are recorded there for ease of checking payments.

A remittance advice is sent with payments from customers so that the supplier is aware of what the cheque or money transfer relates to.

Acceptable methods of payment include:

BACS

Debit card

Credit card

Cheque

Notes and coins

CHAPTER 5
Cash Receipts and Cash Sales

Practice Questions

Chapter 5

5.1

Dawson Supplies keeps an analysed cash book. Money received is entered into the cash book and at the end of the week it is totalled and posted to the main ledger accounts. Dawson Supplies does not have a separate bank account and so the cash book is part of the main ledger. Money is banked at the end of each day which means a separate cash column is not required.

The opening balance on 2nd February 2015 was £650.00

The following transactions took place in February 2015:

2nd Feb	Cheque received from a credit customer R Burch	£616.87
	Cash sale (including VAT)	£960.00
3rd Feb	Cheque received from a credit customer J Kovacs (£50 discount taken)	£293.75
4th Feb	D N'Guessan paid us the rent for the spare office space (No VAT is charged on the rent)	£120.00
	Cash Sale (including VAT)	£624.00
5th Feb	Cash sale (including VAT)	£138.00
	Cheque received from a credit customer F Sinclair (£50 discount taken)	£881.25
6th Feb	Cash sale (including VAT)	£510.00

Enter these transactions into the analysed cash book on the next page and then total the columns.

The accounts are:

R Burch	SL17	J Kovacs	SL29
F Sinclair	SL40		

5.2

Post the cash book totals you calculated in Task 5.1 to the main ledger accounts and the subsidiary ledger accounts. You are not required to show opening balances or to balance any accounts.

CASHBOOK - RECEIPTS **CBR35**

Date	Detail	Folio	Discount Allowed		Bank		Cash Sale		VAT		Sales Ledger		Other Income	
			£	p	£	p	£	p	£	p	£	p	£	p

SALES LEDGER

Dr		R Burch Account (SL 17)			Cr
Date	Details	£	Date	Details	£

Dr		J Kovacs Account (SL 29)			Cr
Date	Details	£	Date	Details	£

Dr	**F Sinclair Account (SL 40)**				Cr
Date	Details	£	Date	Details	£

MAIN LEDGER

Dr	**Sales Account (4000)**				Cr
Date	Details	£	Date	Details	£

Dr	**Rent Received Account (4904)**				Cr
Date	Details	£	Date	Details	£

Dr	**VAT Account (2200)**				Cr
Date	Details	£	Date	Details	£

Dr	**Sales Ledger Control Account (1100)**				Cr
Date	Details	£	Date	Details	£

Dr	**Discounts Allowed Account (4009)**				Cr
Date	Details	£	Date	Details	£

CHAPTER 5
Cash Receipts and Cash Sales

5.3

Examine the following cheque

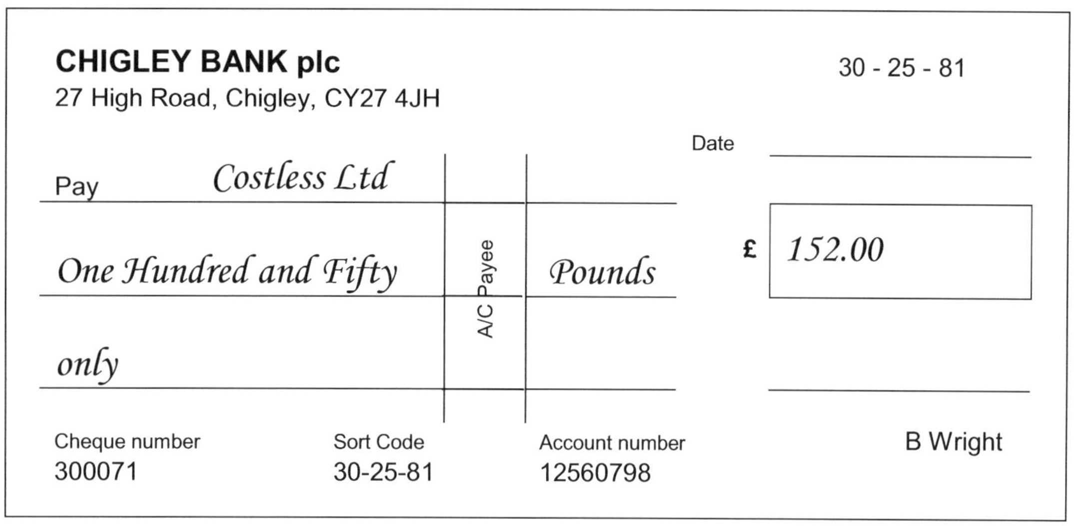

a) Find 3 problems with this cheque

b) Who is the drawee?

c) What does the two lines with A/C Payee mean?

5.4

What is the difference between a debit card and a credit card?

5.5

What do the following stand for:

a) BACS

b) EFTPOS

c) CHAPS

d) FPS?

(This page is left blank for your notes)

Chapter 6

Dealing with Banks

> In this chapter we will looking at the kinds of accounts you can have with banks
>
> We will look briefly at the bank's clearing system
>
> We will find out how to pay cash and cheques into the bank account
>
> We will look at bank statements
>
> We will look at security and procedures for dealing with cash

A **Bank** is a financial institution which accepts deposits and lends these deposits to others. It is a link between those customers who have cash surpluses and those who have cash deficits.

There are **retail banks** which deal with individuals and small businesses, **business banks** which deal with medium to large businesses, **private banks** which provide services to very wealthy individuals, and **investment banks** which deal with trading on the financial markets with transactions in such areas as stocks and shares or commodities. (In this chapter we will be looking at retail banks). Banks are generally owned by shareholders.

A **Building Society** is similar to a bank, but it is owned by its 'members' (i.e. customers). It offers financial services but mainly to personal customers. They will take deposits from their 'members' and offer loans, especially mortgages for the customers to buy their own home. Many Building Societies (but not all) will offer other financial services such as current accounts (see later in this chapter) and savings accounts.

When you open a bank account both you and the bank take on certain rights. As a customer you are required to take reasonable steps to ensure your account doesn't go overdrawn (unless by prior arrangement) and that cheques are written carefully and legibly so that they cannot be altered or misinterpreted. You are also required to check your **statement** (see later in this chapter) to ensure there have been no fraudulent transactions.

The bank, on the other hand has a duty to pay cheques (as long as there are sufficient funds), send regular statements, and to keep the account details secret.

If either customer or bank fails in their duties then charges can be made against the other party and even court action can follow if it is serious enough.

The **basic bank account** is where you can pay cash and cheques into the account and you can take money out either over the counter or with a card at a cash machine. You can also set up **direct debits** and **standing orders** (see previous chapter), so that regular bills will be paid or taken automatically from the account.

The next step up is the **current account**. This offers the same facilities as a basic account, but you will also get a cheque book and probably a debit card. You will also be able to set up standing orders. Perhaps the biggest change is that you can have an **overdraft**, if you arrange it with the bank. An overdraft is a facility whereby you can take out more money from the account than you have put in. If there is prior agreement with the bank and the amount taken out is within the limit agreed then the bank will charge interest at an agreed rate. If there is no agreement or the amount goes over the agreed amount then fees will be charged as well as a higher rate of interest. Many banks will pay interest to the customer where the customer has not used the overdraft facility and there are funds available in the account. Don't expect to get rich on the amount of interest paid, though, as it usually amounts to only a few pence per month. How much will depend on the balance in the account.

There are also many different kinds of **savings account** (sometimes called a **deposit account**). These all pay interest, but different rates and conditions apply. Some require you to keep your money in for a specific term to be able to take advantage of the best rates. You won't get a cheque book or an overdraft with a savings account, but the rates of interest paid are usually much higher than on a current account. Interest from whatever account is usually paid after income tax has been taken, (it is paid for you by the bank, currently at the rate of 20%) although you can apply for interest to be paid without the tax being taken in certain circumstances. Many businesses have both a current account and a savings account, transferring money from the savings account if and when needed.

An overdraft is usually to cover day-to-day expenses and will vary regularly according to the needs of the customer. A **loan** is different in that it is usually used to cover purchases of specific items. The borrower initially receives an amount of money from the bank, which they pay back, usually but not always in regular instalments. This service is generally provided at a cost, referred to as interest.

In all of the above accounts the relationship between the bank and the customer is one of **debtor** and **creditor**. The debtor is the one who owes the money and the creditor is the one who you owe money to.

There are other services offered by the banks. A **mortgage** is the pledging of a property to a lender as a security for a loan. While a mortgage in itself is not a debt, it is evidence of a debt. A mortgage is a document which shows that the customer (**mortgagor**) promises to give the rights of his/her property to the bank (**mortgagee**) until the loan is paid off, or if the mortgagor doesn't keep up the payments.

Banks may also offer services such as arranging insurance or selling shares. The bank may agree to set up an arrangement with a third party such as an insurance company or a stock broker. In these cases the customer is known as the **principal** and the bank is known as the **agent**.

Finally the bank may agree to look after valuable property or documents. The **bailor** is the owner of the property who gives possession (but not ownership) of the goods to the **bailee**.

Cheque clearing

You may already know that if you pay a cheque into your account, you cannot draw on it for 4 working days. The reason for this is best demonstrated by an example.

Cheque clearing system

Day 0 (Monday)

Mr Singh gives a cheque to Mrs Chapman in payment for goods. Mrs Chapman pays the cheque into her bank account on that day. Mrs Chapman's bank will update her account with the amount of the cheque. At the end of the day Mrs Chapman's bank will send all the cheques received to its clearing centre.

Day 1 (Tuesday)

The details of the cheque such as the sort code, account number and the amount of the cheque are sent electronically to the bank on which the cheque is drawn (i.e. Mr Singh's bank). The physical cheque is bundled with all the rest of that bank's cheques and sent to the bank also, via a central exchange centre. In England this centre is in Milton Keynes and in Scotland it is in Edinburgh.

Day 2 (Wednesday)

Mr Singh's account will be updated. He will stop earning interest on the funds. Mrs Chapman will start earning interest on the funds. However, it is still possible for the cheque to be returned due to insufficient funds or if Mr Singh puts a 'stop' on the cheque. As far as the central clearing centre is concerned, Wednesday is the day when the net amount the banks must pay to or receive from each other on the basis of the value of all the cheques exchanged on the previous day is calculated. The net balances are then settled across accounts held at the Bank of England.

Day 4 (Friday)

Mrs Chapman will be able to withdraw funds based on the cheque from her account.

Day 6 (Tuesday)

Mrs Chapman can be certain that the cheque has cleared and that the money is hers.

CHAPTER 6
Dealing with Banks

Paying cash and cheques into a bank

The following page shows an example of a paying in slip. You will notice that both the front and reverse need to be completed.

Date ____________________

Please detail cheques and slips on the back

Cashier's stamp

Bank Giro Credit

IMMINGHAM BANK plc
14 Springfield Road, Brigg, DN20 3GF
Account
Dawson & Co
Paid in by

NUMBER OF CHEQUES/ SLIPS

£50		
£20		
£10		
£5		
£1		
50p		
Silver		
Bronze		
TOTAL CASH		
Cheque/slips		
£		

Sort Code	Account Number
01-26-73	54379654

Paying in slip (front)

Details of cheques/slips	Amount £	p
Total cheques/slips carried over		

Paying in slip (back)

When you open a bank account you will normally be given a **'paying in' book**. Often the paying in slips will be printed at the back of the cheque book, but businesses generally receive a separate paying in book. Some banks provide paying in slips in their foyer, but the account name, sort code, account number and branch name will have to be filled in manually.

To complete a paying in slip you will first need to summarise the different categories of notes and coins being deposited. 'Silver' refers to 20p, 10p and 5p; 'bronze' refers to 2p and 1p.

A summary of the cheques being paid in will be entered on the back with the total entered on the front. The number of cheques is written in the box.

It is increasingly rare nowadays, with credit and debit card transactions being recorded electronically, but if a manual system still exists then a sales voucher will be created. This is paid into the bank the same as a cheque. (These are cleared in a similar way to cheques, but with a card merchant's services).

The person paying in the cash will need to sign the front of the paying in slip.

The slip is given to the cashier at the bank along with the payment.

There is usually a counterfoil in the paying in book so that a record of the payment can be kept by the customer.

Bank statement

A bank will send a statement to its customers at regular intervals. This can be weekly, monthly or even quarterly depending on how much the account is used and how many transactions need to be shown on the statement. It lists deposits, withdrawals, cheques paid, interest earned, and service charges or penalties incurred on the account. It shows the cumulative effect of these transactions in the account's balance, up to the date the report was prepared.

It is essential that a business checks the statement against its own records. This is done by means of a **bank reconciliation** which will be dealt with in detail later in this book. The balance on the statement may not be the same as the balance in the cash book for a number of reasons:

Cheques that the company has written may not have been presented at the bank yet

Cheques may not have completed the clearing system yet

Bank charges may have been made by the bank, but are not yet recorded in the cash book

Interest paid by the bank will not yet be shown in the cash book

Cash and cheques that have been paid into the bank may have been too late for inclusion in the statement.

IMMINGHAM BANK plc
14 Springfield Road, Brigg, DN20 3GF

STATEMENT

Account name: Dawson Supplies Statement no: 132

Account number : 12560798 30-25-81

Date	Details	Payments £	Receipts £	Balance £
2014				
1st Aug	Balance brought forward			1,356.25 O/D
4th Aug	500027	3,250.00		4,606.25 O/D
8th Aug	CC		13,600.27	8,994.02
11th Aug	500028	4,371.19		4,622.83
11th Aug	500030	958.56		3,664.27
15th Aug	CC		6,572.89	10,237.16
15th Aug	500029	5,271.99		4,965.17
18th Aug	DD: Everett Ltd	950.00		4,015.17
22nd Aug	CC		3,751.03	7,766.20
26th Aug	CT: Fry Supplies		7,500.00	15,266.20
29th Aug	CC		2,975.63	18,241.83
29th Aug	Bank Charges	57.39		18,184.44

CC:	Cash and cheques	DD:	Direct Debit
CT:	Credit transfer	O/D	Overdrawn

You will notice that the entries are the opposite way round to the company's cash book. In the statement, payments are on the left and receipts are on the right. This is because the bank statement is written from the bank's point of view and not the company's. A credit entry increases what the bank owes (back to the customer) while a debit entry reduces this amount (cf. p49).

Procedures and security for handling cash

Until the bank receives the cash, it is a security risk. Theft is a real threat and not just from outsiders. There are many instances where money has been taken illegally by company employees.

While it is impossible to completely eradicate the threat of theft, a company can take steps to make it more difficult.

> Receipts from customers making cash purchases should be kept locked away, either in a cash box, or a cash till. If there is no till roll then amounts taken should be recorded manually. The box or till should be closed at all times except when money is actually being used.
>
> The money in the till should be counted at least at the end of every day and compared with the till roll or manually written list. (Remember to account for the float). The cash count should be done by someone who didn't actually take the money, or by two independent people.
>
> Spot checks are sometimes made to ensure that what should be in the till actually is.
>
> Cheques received through the post or over the counter should be recorded on a cash register or some other similar document.
>
> It is preferable to take cash to the bank daily. If this is not possible then a night safe should be used. Some banks also offer the facility of a night safe, where money can be deposited in the bank's safe after the bank has closed. Arrangements should be made for this facility for Friday and weekend takings when the bank is not open.
>
> There should be at least two people taking cash to the bank, or larger companies may make use of a security firm.
>
> When taking money out of the bank (for example to pay wages) again there should be at least two people, or use a security firm.

Once the cash reaches the bank you can be almost certain it is safe. The recent Northern Rock crisis, which saw the first run on a UK bank since Victorian times, did highlight that even in a bank your money is not completely safe, but following these events the government will now guarantee deposits up to £35,000 and there are proposals to increase this limit to £100,000.

Paying cash into the bank as soon as possible is not only a security measure. Cheques sitting in a company's shop cannot be cashed for 4 working days after they have been presented at the bank. This means that the company does not have readily available funds to pay bills and creditors. In addition, the money is not making interest. If there are considerable amounts lying about in the office the lost interest could amount to tens or hundreds of pounds.

When preparing cash for paying into the bank, notes should be sorted so they all face the same way, and coins can be sorted and put into money bags. These are plastic bags which can be obtained from the bank, and it tells you on the bag what amounts are acceptable. In this way completed bags can be weighed rather than counted, which saves a great deal of time.

Cheques should be checked for signature, date (remember it is out of date if it is more than 6 months old), payee, and that words and figures match. A record of the cheques paid in should be kept in case there is a problem, such as the cheque being returned due to insufficient funds.

Chapter Summary

There are many different kinds of bank account.

An overdraft is a method of borrowing money.

Banks offer other services other than just cash transactions. In all cases the relationship between bank and customer have legal terminology.

All cheques must go through the central clearing system. It may take up to 6 working days to ensure that the money from a cheque is yours although funds can normally be drawn after 4 working days.

Money is paid in to a bank by completing a paying in slip.

Banks send regular statements to customers showing all the transactions that have taken place on the account and showing the balance at the end of the period.

Security measures should be in place for handling cash. Cash and cheques should be prepared carefully for taking to the bank.

Practice Questions

Chapter 6

6.1 It is part of your job to count up the cash in the till at the end of the day and to prepare a paying in slip. Today's date is 6th February 2015.

Complete the following table:

Denomination	Quantity	Total £
£50	0	
£20	6	
£10	9	
£5	8	
£1	27	
50p	12	
20p	15	
10p	36	
5p	8	
2p	6	
1p	15	

In addition there are two cheques:

From G Bell £170.00
From N Hussain £500.00

You need to keep a float of £50 for the next day consisting of:

Two £10 notes
Two £5 notes
Ten £1 coins
Ten 50p coins
Fifteen 20p coins
Fifteen 10p coins
Six 5p coins
Five 2p coins
Ten 1p coins

Complete the front and rear of the paying in slip shown on the next page.

Date ______________________

Please detail cheques and slips on the back

Cashier's stamp

Bank Giro Credit

IMMINGHAM BANK plc 14 Springfield Road, Brigg, DN20 3GF	
Account Dawson Supplies	
Paid in by	

	£	p
£50		
£20		
£10		
£5		
£1		
50p		
Silver		
Bronze		
TOTAL CASH		
Cheque/slips		
£		

NUMBER OF CHEQUES/ SLIPS

Sort Code	Account Number
01-26-73	54379654

Paying in slip (front)

Details of cheques/slips	Amount £	p
Total cheques/slips carried over		

Paying in slip (back)

CHAPTER 6
Dealing with Banks

6.2

What is the difference between a loan and an overdraft?

6.3

You are going to open a bank account for your new business. You will need a cheque book and maybe an overdraft facility at some stage in the future. What kind of bank account should you open?

6.4

You receive your bank statement at the end of the month, but you notice that the total on the statement is not the same total as in your cash book. Give 5 reasons why this may be.

Chapter 7

Recording Purchases

> In this chapter we will be looking at how we record a credit purchase in our books.
>
> We will look at recording purchase returns.
>
> We shall see how the documents shown in Chapter 2 are recorded in the books of prime entry and then into the double entry accounts for purchases.
>
> We shall look at the uses of a Purchases Ledger Control account.
>
> We shall review how to balance an account.

Before we can record purchases correctly we must know what a **purchase** is. While this may at first seem quite obvious, in accounting a 'purchase' has a specific meaning. A purchase, for the purpose of keeping books, is buying goods with the intention of selling them as part of the company's trade. So a car sales business would count cars as purchases as it was the intention to sell the cars. However, a van to a grocery store would **not** be a purchase, because the grocery store would not normally trade in vans.

So if you were asked to buy pens, paper, tea or coffee for your office, you would not treat these as 'purchases'. Instead they will be recorded in an equipment, stationery or miscellaneous account. What the account will be called will vary from company to company, but in any event it must **not** be recorded as 'purchases'.

> **LEARNING POINT**
>
> It is a common error in exams to treat the goods bought wrongly. You must be aware that the term 'purchases' can only be attributed to some goods.
>
> Remember that if you are going to sell the goods as your normal trade then it is a 'purchase'. If you are going to use the goods within the company then you will have to use an expense or asset account.

CHAPTER 7

Recording Purchases

Documents involved in making a purchase

Essentially the documents for a purchase are exactly the same as shown for a sale in Chapter 2, except, of course, that you will receive some documents rather than prepare them yourself, and you will send some documents which you received in the sale.

Let us remind ourselves of what documents you are likely to come across:

A catalogue or price list
The buyer will have a catalogue or price list sent (or maybe he/she has seen the price advertised).

A quote
The buyer may receive a quote for the goods.

A purchase order
The buyer will make a firm order for the goods.

A delivery note
The buyer will receive a delivery note with the goods when they arrive. Remember there will be at least two copies of this; one for the buyer and one for the seller. This is so that everyone knows what has been delivered. The signed delivery note becomes proof that the buyer has received the goods.

A goods received note
We haven't come across this document yet in this book. It is a document used by some companies to tell the receiving staff (probably the stores manager) what is expected on the deliveries.

DAWSON SUPPLIES

45 Scartho Street, Immingham, IM15 2BH

Goods Received Note

From: **Halls Ltd**

Descripton of item(s)	Quanitity	Received in good condition?
Blue Cotton Dress Material	50 rolls	

Signed   Date:

You can see that the goods received note is an internal document. The goods expected will already appear on the document. It is up to the receiving person to complete the 'Received in good condition?' boxes and to sign and date it. It will be used by the accounts department as a check that the correct goods have been received and that they are in good condition so that the invoice can be paid when the time comes.

An invoice
The buyer will receive an invoice from the seller sometimes at the same time as the goods are delivered, but more usually in the post a day or so later. Remember that you should **never** pay an invoice until you are authorised to do so. Many companies will either have someone to sign the invoice ready for payment or it will be rubber stamped. Some companies pay invoices when they receive the statement while others will pay after the maximum number of days allowed.

A returns note
Another document we haven't touched on in this book yet. It will accompany any faulty goods which need to be sent back to the seller. It simply lists what has been returned and gives the reason for the return.

A credit note
This is sent by the seller to the buyer to reduce the amount of the invoice due to faulty goods having been returned.

LEARNING POINT

Make sure that you never alter an invoice from a supplier. This can lead to great problems with the accounting records and even have the seller and the buyer recording the invoice with different figures.

Always ask for a credit note, even if it is for the whole amount on the invoice. Then the buyer and the seller are sure what has been accepted and what has been returned and can record it correctly in their books.

A statement of account
This is received by the buyer and lets him/her know how much is owing and when. The buyer will check the statement against his/her own records.

A remittance advice
When the buyer does eventually pay the invoice(s) he/she will send a remittance advice showing what the payment is for. This is vital so that both seller and buyer know exactly what has been paid for and what is still outstanding.

If you are not sure about any of these documents you may want to return to Chapter 2. You **will** come across most of them in your exams and in your later studies so you need to know what they look like and what they are for. You will need to check that they have suitable signatures and the calculations are correct. If there are any problems you will need to refer them either back to the supplier, or to your manager.

LEARNING POINT

In your exam you may be asked to prepare invoices for payment. This will mean that you will have to check:

Goods received note to delivery note

Delivery note to purchase order

Invoice to purchase order, delivery note and goods received note

You may not have all the above documents, but you will have to refer discrepancies and remember that an unsigned document doesn't show anything. If it's not signed it's not valid.

You should remember that getting the VAT right is up to the supplier. As long as the invoice is valid in other ways your choice is to pay an incorrect amount of VAT or to refer it back to the supplier. You **will** be able to claim the VAT back whatever the amount with a valid invoice.

You must also check that the invoice has been authorised for payment before you pay it.

Not all of the above documents are used by every business. Purchases can be made over the phone or by fax. Electronic communication also makes some of the documents redundant. There are two main types of electronic trading; **e-commerce** which is basically trading over the internet, and **EDI**. EDI stands for Electronic Data Interchange and is where businesses are linked by computer so that purchase orders, invoices and payments can be made electronically. Don't confuse EDI with the internet. EDI is a more secure link between businesses.

Recording purchases made on credit

There is not a great deal of difference in recording a purchase on credit to recording a sale on credit except that the entries are on the opposite side of the accounts. We will look at this next. First we will look at the **purchases day book**. Like the sales day book, it is a book of prime entry, meaning that this is the first place that invoices received will be recorded.

PURCHASES DAY BOOK **PDB 23**

Date	Invoice	Supplier	Folio	Total		Purchases Clothes		Other expenses		VAT	
2014				£	p	£	p	£	p	£	p
01 Sep	23579	L Wilkinson	PL 31	600	00	500	00			100	00
08 Sep	1479	M Ahmed	PL 05	420	00	350	00			70	00
15 Sep	36758	Immingham Phones	PL 12	87	07			72	56	14	51
22 Sep	A652	Powell Motors	PL 21	311	82			259	85	51	97
29 Sep	2975	R Singh	PL 28	750	60	625	50			125	10
30 Sep		**TOTAL FOR THE MONTH**		**2169**	**49**	**1475**	**50**	**332**	**41**	**361**	**58**

Let us look at the details of the purchases day book. Remember that each invoice the company receives will be recorded here first.

PDB 23 stands for Purchases Day Book page 23. Codes are essential for easy reference. If you are using a computer you cannot do without codes.

The date is the date of the invoice.

The invoice number is taken from the actual invoice. Some companies may give a code number to each invoice they receive. This may be used here instead according to company policy.

The 'folio' refers to the code given to each supplier. Here PL stands for Purchases Ledger and the number of the account for that supplier.

The total amount of the invoice is then shown.

The next two columns are essential. This categorises the goods bought into either 'purchases' or 'expenses'. Many companies will have more analysis columns so that the expenses can be categorised more specifically. Typical examples are 'motor expenses', 'advertising', 'telephone', 'cleaning'. Remember that each column of the analysis will need its own account in the books.

The net amount is put into the columns. You may be able to take this from the invoice or you may have to calculate the net amount (see p 37).

Finally the amount of VAT will be recorded.

LEARNING POINT

You must remember that just because there is a box in the purchases day book, it doesn't have to have anything in it.

You should always check your adding up. Look at the totals across the bottom. You will see that £361.58 + £332.41 + £1475.50 = £2169.49. This calculation ensures that your figures **cross-cast**.

Now let us see how this is recorded in our double entry.

First we record each invoice in the individual customer accounts in our **purchases ledger**.

PURCHASES LEDGER

Dr		**L Wilkinson Account (PL 31)**			Cr
Date	Details	£	Date	Details	£
			01/09/14	PDB 23	600.00

Dr		**M Ahmed Account (PL 05)**			Cr
Date	Details	£	Date	Details	£
			08/09/14	PDB 23	420.00

Dr	Immingham Phones Account (PL 12)				Cr
Date	Details	£	Date	Details	£
			15/09/14	PDB 23	87.07

Dr	Powell Motors Account (PL 21)				Cr
Date	Details	£	Date	Details	£
			22/09/14	PDB 23	311.82

Dr	R Singh Account (PL 28)				Cr
Date	Details	£	Date	Details	£
			29/09/14	PDB 23	750.60

Then there are the entries in the main ledger

MAIN LEDGER

Dr	Purchases (Clothes)				Cr
Date	Details	£	Date	Details	£
30/09/14	PDB 23	1475.50			

Dr	Other expenses				Cr
Date	Details	£	Date	Details	£
30/09/14	PDB 23	332.41			

Dr		VAT Account			Cr
Date	Details	£	Date	Details	£
30/09/14	PDB 23	361.58			

The most important thing to note is that the entries are all on the other side of the accounts to the sales. In all other respects it is the same. You should still note that the total of all the debits equals the total of all the credits. The principle of debits for 'receiving' and credits for 'giving' is still maintained.

Just as before with sales, many companies will summarise their Purchases Ledger in a **Purchases Ledger Control account**. If this is done then the main ledger will look as follows:

MAIN LEDGER

Dr		Purchases (Clothes)			Cr
Date	Details	£	Date	Details	£
30/09/14	PDB 23	1475.50			

Dr		Other expenses			Cr
Date	Details	£	Date	Details	£
30/09/14	PDB 23	332.41			

Dr		VAT Account			Cr
Date	Details	£	Date	Details	£
30/09/14	PDB 23	361.58			

Dr	Purchases Ledger Control Account				Cr
Date	Details	£	Date	Details	£
			30/09/14	PDB 23	2169.49

Remember that the Purchases Ledger will look exactly the same as before but it won't be part of the double entry.

Purchases returns

When we receive a credit note it will be entered into the **Purchases Returns Day Book**.

PURCHASES RETURNS DAY BOOK **PRDB 03**

Date	Cr Note	Supplier	Folio	Total		Purchases Clothes		Other Expenses		VAT	
2014				£	p	£	p	£	p	£	p
03 Sep	C237	L Wilkinson	PL 31	60	00	50	00			10	00
10 Sep	0793	M Ahmed	PL 05	120	00	100	00			20	00
30 Sep		**TOTAL FOR THE MONTH**		**180**	**00**	**150**	**00**	**0**	**00**	**30**	**00**

Remember to make sure your figures cross-cast again.

Then you will transfer the amounts to the Purchases Ledger and the Main Ledger.

When you have done this your accounts should look like this:

PURCHASES LEDGER

Dr	L Wilkinson Account (PL 31)				Cr
Date	Details	£	Date	Details	£
03/09/14	**PRDB 03**	**60.00**	01/09/14	PDB 23	600.00

Dr	M Ahmed Account (PL 05)				Cr
Date	Details	£	Date	Details	£
10/09/14	**PRDB 03**	**120.00**	08/09/14	PDB 23	420.00

Dr	Immingham Phones Account (PL 12)				Cr
Date	Details	£	Date	Details	£
			15/09/14	PDB 23	87.07

Dr	Powell Motors Account (PL 21)				Cr
Date	Details	£	Date	Details	£
			22/09/14	PDB 23	311.82

Dr	R Singh Account (PL 28)				Cr
Date	Details	£	Date	Details	£
			29/09/14	PDB 23	750.60

Then there are the entries in the main ledger

MAIN LEDGER

Dr		Purchases (Clothes)			Cr
Date	Details	£	Date	Details	£
30/09/14	PDB 23	1475.50			

Dr		Purchases Returns Account (Clothes)			Cr
Date	Details	£	Date	Details	£
			30/09/14	**PRDB 03**	**150.00**

Dr		Other expenses			Cr
Date	Details	£	Date	Details	£
30/09/14	PDB 23	332.41			

Dr		VAT Account			Cr
Date	Details	£	Date	Details	£
30/09/14	PDB 23	361.58	**30/09/14**	**PRDB 03**	**30.00**

Dr		Purchases Ledger Control Account			Cr
Date	Details	£	Date	Details	£
03/09/14	**PRDB 03**	**180.00**	30/09/14	PDB 23	2169.49

LEARNING POINT

One of the important things to learn is what amount goes in what account. Many marks are lost by students by putting net amounts in the individual customer accounts and the Purchases Ledger Control.

Make sure you learn that the gross amount goes in the Purchases Ledger and Purchases Ledger Control and the net amount goes in the Purchases account and the Purchases Returns account.

This rule holds good for the sales side of the accounts.

Batch control system

Some companies use a batch control system. This is particularly useful when a computer is being used to enter data. The batch control is similar to a day book and is used instead of it. All the invoices for (say) purchases will be listed and totalled. The computer operator will then be able to enter all the invoices in one run without having to skip from one part of the computer program to another. When all the invoices have been recorded the total is checked to the batch total. Discrepancies must be investigated at once. This can be done for both purchases invoices and sales invoices

Balancing accounts

On p62 you learnt how to balance accounts. A similar process takes place with the purchases accounts. If you can't remember how to balance the accounts go back and review the process. In the exam you **will** be expected to know this process.

Here are two of the above supplier accounts which have been balanced

Dr	**L Wilkinson Account (PL 31)**				Cr
Date	Details	£	Date	Details	£
03/09/14	PRDB 03	60.00	01/09/14	PDB 23	600.00
30/09/14	**Balance c/d**	**540.00**			
		600.00			**600.00**
			01/10/14	**Balance b/d**	**540.00**

Dr	**M Ahmed Account (PL 05)**				Cr
Date	Details	£	Date	Details	£
10/09/14	PRDB 03	120.00	08/09/14	PDB 23	420.00
30/09/14	**Balance c/d**	**300.00**			
		420.00			**420.00**
			01/10/14	**Balance b/d**	**300.00**

Chapter Summary

'Purchases' only relate to some of the items a company buys.

Documents for making purchases are the same documents used in a sale except that the company receives them rather than sends them.

All documents should be signed and any figures should be checked for accuracy.

Purchase invoices are first recorded in the Purchases Day Book.

'Totals' figures should be checked for accuracy.

Invoices are recorded in the Purchases Ledger and in the relevant main ledger accounts.

A Purchase Ledger Control account is a summary of the Purchases Ledger. If a company uses a Purchases Ledger Control account then the individual customer accounts will not then be part of the double entry.

Credit Notes received are recorded in the Purchases Returns Day Book and then the amounts are transferred to the relevant accounts in the Purchases Ledger and the main ledger.

When accounts are prepared on computer a system of batch control may be used.

Accounts must be balanced at regular intervals.

CHAPTER 7
Recording Purchases

Practice Questions

Chapter 7

7.1
Put the following documents in the order they would be used:

i) Invoice
ii) Purchase order
iii) Statement of account
iv) Delivery note
v) Remittance Advice

7.2
Today is 6th February 2015. You work in a company which sells electrical goods. You receive the following invoices from your credit suppliers:

Invoice 23571 from L Butler	10 Microwaves £600.00 including VAT
Invoice 7596 from B Knight	15 Electric Kettles £540.00 including VAT
Invoice 3964 from M Barnes	10 Toasters £240.00 including VAT
Invoice 93678 from H Lloyd	10 Reams photocopy paper £60.00 including VAT
Invoice 57465 from D Mills	5 Cappuccino Makers £330.00 including VAT

Purchases Ledger account numbers

M Barnes	PL 7	H Lloyd	PL 31
L Butler	PL 15	D Mills	PL 46
B Knight	PL 25		

Enter the transactions into the purchases day book on the next page
Total the purchases day book
Post the entries to the main and subsidiary ledgers on the following pages

7.3
It is now 9th February 2015. You receive the following credit notes:

Credit Note CN 537 from M Barnes	2 Toasters (damaged) £48.00 including VAT
Credit Note RT 335 from B Knight	1 Electric Kettle (faulty) £36.00 including VAT

Enter the transactions into the purchases returns day book
Total the purchases returns day book and post the entries into the same accounts you used for task 7.2

Balance the accounts

PURCHASES DAY BOOK **PDB 57**

Date	Invoice	Supplier	Folio	Total		Purchases		Other expenses		VAT	
				£	p	£	p	£	p	£	p
		TOTAL									

PURCHASES RETURNS DAY BOOK **PRDB 03**

Date	Cr Note	Supplier	Folio	Total		Purchases returns		Other returns		VAT	
				£	p	£	p	£	p	£	p
		TOTAL									

CHAPTER 7
Recording Purchases

PURCHASES LEDGER

Dr			M Barnes Account (PL 7)		Cr
Date	Details	£	Date	Details	£

Dr			L Butler Account (PL 15)		Cr
Date	Details	£	Date	Details	£

Dr			B Knight Account (PL 25)		Cr
Date	Details	£	Date	Details	£

Dr			H Lloyd Account (PL 31)		Cr
Date	Details	£	Date	Details	£

Dr			D Mills Account (PL 46)		Cr
Date	Details	£	Date	Details	£

MAIN LEDGER

Dr		Purchases			Cr
Date	Details	£	Date	Details	£

Dr		Purchases Returns			Cr
Date	Details	£	Date	Details	£

Dr		Other expenses			Cr
Date	Details	£	Date	Details	£

Dr		VAT Account			Cr
Date	Details	£	Date	Details	£

Dr		Purchases Ledger Control Account			Cr
Date	Details	£	Date	Details	£

(This page is left blank for your notes)

Chapter 8

Making Payments

> In this chapter we will be looking at how we can make payments and when.
>
> We will look at recording payments in the cash book
>
> We shall see how to post the cash book entries
>
> We shall see how to reconcile the Purchases Ledger Control account
>
> We will look at what may happen when the same company is both a customer and a supplier.

All businesses need to pay for their purchases at some time. The timing may be critical to the organisation. If invoices are paid immediately when a 30 day credit has been offered, then 30 days of interest from the cash in the bank will be lost. This may not be a lot of money on just a few payments, but imagine a company with hundreds of payments covering millions of pounds.

Each company will have its own policy on when to pay invoices. For example it may be more beneficial to take a settlement discount and pay early rather than take the interest from the bank and pay later. (You will learn how to calculate the benefits of this, later in your studies). Looking at this from the seller's point of view, you can probably see that offering credit costs a company money in lost interest. This lost interest will be taken into account when deciding how much products will sell for, and it is essential that procedures are in place to avoid buyers taking longer credit than they are entitled to.

Whenever you pay your money, you must make certain checks before any money leaves the company or the company's bank account.

1. Check all the relevant documentation. The Purchase Order should match the Delivery Note and the Goods Received Note (if there is one) and they should all match the Invoice. Remember that a document is not valid unless it is dated and signed by an authorised signatory.

2. If goods have been returned to the supplier, then a Credit Note must have been received before payment is made.

3. Payment must be adjusted for any discounts. The invoice will show any trade or bulk discount, but you must make sure it is there if your company is entitled to it. Mistakes may not be rectified later. You must also allow for any settlement

discount if you are entitled to it. The amount may not be shown on the invoice so you may have to calculate the amount yourself. Don't expect a supplier to rush to give you your money back if you've paid too much!

4. Payments must receive the necessary authorisation. Often the invoice will be signed or rubber stamped by a supervisor when payment can be paid. Other companies will initial those items on a statement of account which can be paid. Always check that the proper authority has been given and that the authority is from the person authorised to do so.

Remember that payment by cheque or BACS should be accompanied by a remittance advice. This is particularly important for a BACS payment as without the remittance advice the supplier will not know that anything has been paid at all.

Payment to suppliers will usually have a regular procedure. Less regular payments are usually requested on a **Cheque Requisition Form**.

DAWSON SUPPLIES

CHEQUE REQUISITION FORM

CHEQUE PAYABLE TO : - ....

Details	Expenditure code	£	p
	Total		

Requested by :-	Date:-
Authorised by:-	
Finance use only	
Cheque number :-	
Date :-	

Deadline date of processing cheque :- ....

CHAPTER 8
Making Payments

Cheque requisition forms are used for requesting cheques for such items as new office equipment (perhaps a new computer or printer), or for placing an advertisement in the local paper. They are to be used if someone needs to be reimbursed for expenses over a certain amount which is decided by the company. (Smaller amounts will be processed through the Petty Cash as we shall see later in this book). The Payee must provide receipts that exactly make up the total needing to be reimbursed and the receipts and any other backing documentation that relates to this reimbursement should accompany the form.

A cheque requisition form is essential in larger companies as it is their means of controlling costs and ensuring that what has been bought has been authorised.

Bank Giro Credit

Another form of payment we haven't looked at yet is the Bank Giro Credit. We have touched on this when we have paid cash and cheques into our own bank. The Bank Giro Credit allows money to be paid in at one bank or branch and processed through a clearing system, similar to the cheque clearing system, to another bank or branch. You will have probably seen Bank Giro Credit forms at the bottom of utility bills and credit card bills.

You must remember that the form is not a payment in itself. The form must be accompanied by the payment in the form of cash or a cheque, but it does mean that you can pay some bills simply by visiting your bank.

Other methods of payments

We have already looked at some forms of payment. Standing Orders are covered on p 90. BACS autopay can be used where regular payments are made to multiple accounts. This is ideal for wages and making payments at the end of each month to established suppliers. Once the autopay is set up the company need only supply the bank with the name and amount of payment and the money will be transferred from the company account to the recipient account automatically. The list of payees can be taken, faxed or even phoned to the bank.

Companies can supply their employees with company credit cards. Typically these are used by travelling sales representatives for rail fares, car fuel, accommodation and food, although other employees may be issued them also. The bill will then come from the credit card company at the end of the month. Since an itemised list of purchases will accompany the bill, the employee's expenses can be monitored.

Direct Debits could at one time only be set up by written authority by the customer. A form was completed with the customer's bank details and then sent to the supplier. The supplier would then send the form to his/her bank and that bank would then send the form to the customer's bank. This method takes quite some time to set up and open to delay. As a result BACS allowed a direct debit to be set up electronically. The electronic set up is called **AUDDIS** (Automated Direct Debit Instruction Service). With effect from 1st

January 2008, the use of AUDDIS to submit Direct Debit Instructions is mandatory for all new service users.

Online banking has become very popular. As well as being able to manage your own bank account, online banking allows the customer to make payments to suppliers and to set up standing orders. Regular transfers can also be set up.

CHAPS, FPS, Postal Orders and Banker's drafts have all been covered earlier in this book.

Recording payments

In Chapter 5 we saw how the cash book was both a book of prime entry **and** part of the double entry system. Let us remind ourselves of what a cash book looks like:

CASH BOOK

RECEIPTS | PAYMENTS

Date	Detail	Cash £	Bank £	Date	Detail	Cash £	Bank £

You will remember that receipts go on the left and payments on the right. In this chapter we will look at the payments side of the cash book.

You will remember that the cash book receipts side often has columns which analyse what the receipt is for. The same is true for the payments side. It is often the case that the payments side has more analysis columns than the receipts side as companies usually buy more varied goods and services than they sell. For example the payments side of the cash book may have analysis columns for motor expenses, stationery, cleaning, travel, etc. each of which will have its own account. This means that a manual cash book can be quite a large book with a page on the left for the receipts and a page on the right for payments.

For simplicity, we will not have many expense accounts here and we will put them all together under the heading of 'Other Expenses'. You must remember that it is likely that a company cash book will have many more columns than shown here.

Let us look at some typical entries on the payments side of the analysed cash book.

CASHBOOK - PAYMENTS CBP35

Date	Detail	Folio	Discount Received		Bank		Cash Purchases		VAT		Purchases Ledger		Other Expenses	
			£	p	£	p	£	p	£	p	£	p	£	p
01/10/14	Cash Purchase	ML			600	00	500	00	100	00				
08/10/14	M Ahmed	PL	10	00	290	00					290	00		
15/10/14	Rent	ML			95	25							95	25
22/10/14	C Kaur	PL			534	96					534	96		
29/10/14	Wages	ML			525	50							525	50
30/10/14	Cash Purchase	ML			360	00	300	00	60	00				
			10	**00**	**2405**	**71**	**800**	**00**	**160**	**00**	**824**	**96**	**620**	**75**

Firstly you will notice that there is no cash column. Obviously this means the company keeps limited cash on the premises and doesn't pay bill with notes and coins on a regular basis, although there may be petty cash for small items. (See later in this book).

There is no balance b/d. This is shown on the other side of the cash book as the company either doesn't have, or has not used an overdraft facility. Had there been a balance b/d here then the payments from previous periods would have exceeded the receipts and so the credit balance would have shown that the company was overdrawn.

The cash purchase on 1st October would have been for goods bought for resale. (See p 113 for an explanation of the meaning of a 'purchase'). The total amount paid was £600.00, being £500.00 for the actual goods and £100.00 VAT. Remember that if we are **not** registered for VAT then we couldn't claim the VAT back and we would have no need to record it. The full amount would be recorded in the cash purchases column.

The payment to M Ahmed was payment in respect of a previous invoice. The amount of the goods and any VAT due would have been recorded when the invoice was received, so we must not record the payment as a purchase as it's already been accounted for. However, we have taken a discount of £10. The invoice would have been for £300.00 (or the balance of the invoice if a credit has been received), so the payment has been reduced by the discount amount.

LEARNING POINT

Only **settlement** discounts are recorded in the accounts as these are the only discounts which may or may not be taken. Trade and bulk discounts are not in any doubt as these are given as a matter of course at the time of the sale and so do not play any part in changes to the sale price of the goods or services.

The rent is probably a regular payment. There would have been no invoice or the amount would have been shown as payment against this invoice in the purchases ledger. There is no VAT payable so the whole amount is shown in the 'Other Expenses' column. (Remember that some cash books will have more analysis columns than this and this amount would be shown in the 'rent' column).

The payment to C Kaur is another payment to one of our creditors. This time there is no discount taken and so the invoice would have been for the whole amount of £534.96. We don't want to know the VAT amount as this would have been recorded when the invoice was received in the Purchases Day Book and the main ledger accounts would have been updated at this time. All we want to know now is who was paid and how much.

We will look at wages in more detail in the next chapter, but for now we can see that net wages of £525.50 have been paid from the bank. Again there would probably be a 'wages' column but for now we are grouping all expenses into an 'Other Expenses' account to simplify the process.

The final entry is another cash purchase just the same as the first entry. Remember that it's not important who we buy the goods from as we will not owe them anything. The purchase is complete when the money is handed over.

When you total the cash book at the end of the period you should always check your calculations. The sum of the totals of the analysis columns should equal the Bank column total. As mentioned previously, the discounts column is not strictly a cash book figure. It is there as a memorandum figure only. As such it is not included when your are checking the cross-casting. In our cash book £800.00 + £160.00 + £824.96 + £620.75 = £2405.71

Completing the double entry

So now let's look at the other side of the double entry for each of the cash book entries.

The cash purchases will be dealt with similar to cash sales except all the entries will be on the other side of the accounts.

Dr		Purchases Account			Cr
Date	Details	£	Date	Details	£
31/10/14	CBP35	800.00			

Dr		VAT Account			Cr
Date	Details	£	Date	Details	£
31/10/14	CBP35	160.00			

Remember that the whole £960.00 would be shown in the purchases account if we are not registered for VAT.

Purchases are a debit entry because this is what we are receiving. The total amount is entered rather than one at a time. One at a time would be time consuming and unnecessary. The cash book tells us what we have paid to whom; now all we want to know is how much we have bought in total.

Now let us look at the two payments to suppliers; M Ahmed and C Kaur.

First let's look at how we left M Ahmed's account on p 124.

Dr		M Ahmed Account (PL 05)			Cr
Date	Details	£	Date	Details	£
10/09/14	PRDB 03	120.00	08/09/14	PDB 23	420.00
30/09/14	Balance c/d	300.00			
		420.00			420.00
			01/10/14	Balance b/d	300.00

So now we have to debit this account with the amount that we paid.

LEARNING POINT

While there are other ways of recording this, the one you should use in your exam is to only record the **amount paid** in the creditor's account. You should deal with the discount separately.

Dr	M Ahmed Account (PL 05)				Cr
Date	Details	£	Date	Details	£
10/09/14	PRDB 03	120.00	08/09/14	PDB 23	420.00
30/09/14	Balance c/d	300.00			
		420.00			420.00
08/10/14	**CBP35**	**290.00**	01/10/14	Balance b/d	300.00

If we were to balance this account now then we would see that there would still be a £10.00 credit balance. As we know, a credit balance means that we owe the creditor, but in actual fact we don't owe him/her anything, because we have taken a £10.00 discount. Therefore we need to update our accounts with the discount.

Dr	M Ahmed Account (PL 05)				Cr
Date	Details	£	Date	Details	£
10/09/14	PRDB 03	120.00	08/09/14	PDB 23	420.00
30/09/14	Balance c/d	300.00			
		420.00			420.00
08/10/14	CBP35	290.00	01/10/14	Balance b/d	300.00
08/10/14	**Disc Received**	**10.00**			

Now if we balance the account you will see there is no balance to bring down. We will balance all the accounts in a moment when we have completed **posting** (in accounting terms entering is known as posting) all the figures.

C Kaur's account is one we haven't seen yet so let us imagine it looked like this at the beginning of October.

Dr	C Kaur Account (PL 12)				Cr
Date	Details	£	Date	Details	£
			01/10/14	Balance b/d	872.95

There would be previous entries to this which would have left the balance at £872.95. It would probably have been made up of several invoices and maybe credit notes too. The entry to make here is quite simple as there are no discounts to account for. The invoices we are paying will be shown in the remittance advice we send with our payment.

Dr		C Kaur Account (PL 12)			Cr
Date	Details	£	Date	Details	£
22/10/14	**CBP35**	**534.96**	01/10/14	Balance b/d	872.95

Again we will balance this account later.

So far we have not posted the double entry as these creditor accounts are in the Subsidiary Purchases Ledger. The Purchases Ledger Control account, (which as you will remember is the summary of the accounts in the Purchases Ledger) will need to be updated for this.

Here is how we left it on p 123.

Dr		Purchases Ledger Control Account			Cr
Date	Details	£	Date	Details	£
03/09/14	PRDB 03	180.00	30/09/14	PDB 23	2169.49

Let us now balance it as it should have been at the end of September, and then add the entries from the cash book.

Dr		Purchases Ledger Control Account			Cr
Date	Details	£	Date	Details	£
03/09/14	PRDB 03	180.00	30/09/14	PDB 23	2169.49
30/09/14	Balance c/d	1989.49			
		2169.49			2169.49
31/10/14	**CBP35**	**824.96**	01/10/14	Balance b/d	1989.49
31/10/14	**Disc Received**	**10.00**			

Here it is important to remember to add the discounts received. However, as explained before the discount is not strictly a cashbook transaction. Being only a memorandum column it will need its own double entry. We record the other side of the discount received in (not surprisingly) a Discounts Received account.

Dr		Discounts Received Account			Cr
Date	Details	£	Date	Details	£
			31/10/14	**CBP35**	**10.00**

So now all we are left with is the payment for rent and the wages. As mentioned before these would probably each have their own account, but for simplicity we will just use an 'Other Expenses' account.

Dr		Other expenses			Cr
Date	Details	£	Date	Details	£
31/10/14	**CBP35**	**620.75**			

Notice again how it is the total figure we take and not each individual cashbook entry. For our accounts we only want to see the total.

So now all we have left to do is to balance the accounts. Strictly speaking you should follow the principle for **all** accounts, but it is often the case that accounts with just one entry is left alone. The important thing is that you **follow company procedure**.

In the examples above we only have the Purchases Ledger accounts and The Purchases ledger Control account with more than one entry so we will only balance these.

Dr		M Ahmed Account (PL 05)			Cr
Date	Details	£	Date	Details	£
10/09/14	PRDB 03	120.00	08/09/14	PDB 23	420.00
30/09/14	Balance c/d	300.00			
		420.00			420.00
08/10/14	CBP35	290.00	01/10/14	Balance b/d	300.00
08/10/14	Disc Received	10.00			
		300.00			**300.00**

Here, since there is no balance to carry down, it can be left like this. It is not necessary to show £0.00. Obviously a zero balance is neither a debit nor a credit.

Dr		C Kaur Account (PL 12)			Cr
Date	Details	£	Date	Details	£
22/10/14	CBP35	534.96	01/10/14	Balance b/d	872.95
31/10/14	**Balance c/d**	**337.99**			
		872.95			**872.95**
			01/11/14	**Balance b/d**	**337.99**

Dr	Purchases Ledger Control Account				Cr
Date	Details	£	Date	Details	£
03/09/14	PRDB 03	180.00	30/09/14	PDB 23	2169.49
30/09/14	Balance c/d	1989.49			
		2169.49			2169.49
31/10/14	CBP35	824.96	01/10/14	Balance b/d	1989.49
31/10/14	Disc Received	10.00			
31/10/14	**Balance c/d**	**1154.53**			
		1989.49			**1989.49**
			01/11/14	**Balance b/d**	**1154.53**

If you were not sure how these accounts were balanced then revise the process on p 63 of this book.

Purchases Ledger Control reconciliation

Once we have balanced all the Purchases Ledger accounts and the Purchases Ledger Control account, we can then reconcile them. We saw on p 57 how to reconcile the Sales Ledger Control. Now we need to do exactly the same with our Purchases Ledger Control.

Suppose these are our supplier accounts:

PURCHASES LEDGER

Dr	J Kovacs Account				Cr
Date	Details	£	Date	Details	£
30/11/14	Cash Book	148.00	01/11/14	Balance b/d	150.00
30/11/14	Disc Received	2.00	02/11/14	Purchases	200.00
30/11/14	Balance c/d	200.00			
		350.00			350.00
			01/12/14	Balance b/d	200.00

Dr	D N'Guessan Account				Cr
Date	Details	£	Date	Details	£
30/11/14	Purch Returns	50.00	01/11/14	Balance b/d	300.00
30/11/14	Cash book	250.00	02/11/14	Purchases	450.00
30/11/14	Balance c/d	450.00			
		750.00			750.00
			01/12/14	Balance b/d	450.00

Dr		R Burch Account			Cr
Date	Details	£	Date	Details	£
30/11/14	Purch Returns	100.00	01/11/14	Balance b/d	450.00
30/11/14	Cash book	250.00	02/11/14	Purchases	450.00
30/11/14	Balance c/d	550.00			
		900.00			900.00
			01/12/14	Balance b/d	550.00

Dr		L John-Lewis Account			Cr
Date	Details	£	Date	Details	£
30/11/14	Cash Book	246.00	01/11/14	Balance b/d	600.00
30/11/14	Disc Received	4.00	02/11/14	Purchases	250.00
30/11/14	Balance c/d	600.00			
		850.00			850.00
			01/12/14	Balance b/d	600.00

Now let's look at the Purchases Ledger Control account

Dr		Purchases Ledger Control Account			Cr
Date	Details	£	Date	Details	£
30/11/14	Purch Returns	150.00	01/11/14	Balance b/d	1500.00
30/11/14	Cash Book	894.00	02/11/14	Purchases	1350.00
30/11/14	Balance c/d	1806.00			
		2850.00			2850.00
			01/12/14	Balance b/d	1806.00

Now we can go ahead with our reconciliation

Reconciliation of Purchases Ledger Control Account
31st November 2014

	£	£
J Kovacs	200.00	
D N'Guessan	450.00	
R Burch	550.00	
L John-Lewis	600.00	
TOTAL	**1800.00**	
TOTAL PER PURCHASES LEDGER CONTROL		**1806.00**
Discrepancy (if any)	6.00	

Here we can immediately see that something is wrong. If this happens you must investigate immediately. In this case it appears that the discounts received have been omitted from the Purchases Ledger Control account. It will need putting right, but don't just cross out or add in. In accounting, **journals** are used to correct errors. We will look at journals later in this book. Crossings out or figures added in without explanation gives ample opportunity for fraud, and an auditor would not be happy with unexplained alterations (not to mention your manager!).

Contra entries

Sometimes a business can be both a supplier and a customer at the same time. Let us suppose that Asco Ltd both sells us goods and we sell goods to them. The individual accounts may look like this:

SALES LEDGER

Dr		**Asco Ltd Account**			Cr
Date	Details	£	Date	Details	£
01/11/14	Balance b/d	600.00			

PURCHASES LEDGER

Dr		**Asco Ltd Account**			Cr
Date	Details	£	Date	Details	£
			01/11/14	Balance b/d	800.00

Asco Ltd would have to send us a cheque for £600.00 and we would have to send them one for £800.00. This seems a waste of time and effort with cheques going backward and forwards between the companies, particularly if this happens regularly.

To save the time and effort, with Asco Ltd's agreement, we can set-off one account with the other. A **contra** entry can be made so that one cheque will be all that is required.

The entry would look like those on the next page, with the date being when the agreement was made. The details show where the other side of the contra entry can found (PL stands for Purchases Ledger and SL stands for Sales Ledger).

SALES LEDGER

Dr		Asco Ltd Account			Cr
Date	Details	£	Date	Details	£
01/11/14	Balance b/d	600.00	12/11/14	Contra PL	600.00

PURCHASES LEDGER

Dr		Asco Ltd Account			Cr
Date	Details	£	Date	Details	£
12/11/14	Contra SL	600.00	01/11/14	Balance b/d	800.00

When we come to balance the accounts we can see that the Sales Ledger account has a balance of zero and the Purchases Ledger account has a balance of £200.00. Therefore, to settle both accounts, all that is needed is that we send a cheque for £200.00 to Asco Ltd. Of course, if the Sales Ledger account had been more than the Purchases Ledger account then a cheque would be needed from Asco Ltd rather than from us.

You must remember that these accounts will probably be subsidiary accounts so we must update the Sales Ledger Control (SLC) and the Purchases Ledger Control (PLC).

Dr		Sales Ledger Control Account			Cr
Date	Details	£	Date	Details	£
			12/11/14	Contra PLC	600.00

Dr		Purchases Ledger Control Account			Cr
Date	Details	£	Date	Details	£
12/11/14	Contra SLC	600.00			

The net result is that the amount owing from one to the other is reduced by £600.00 for both Asco Ltd and our company.

LEARNING POINT

It is a good idea to remember which side of the accounts a contra goes. A contra will **always** be on the credit side of the Sales Ledger account and the Sales ledger Control account and it will **always** be on the debit side of the Purchases Ledger account and the Purchases Ledger Control account.

Chapter Summary

Payments must only be paid according to company policy. Documentation must be checked for accuracy and signature.

A payment for unusual or less common items is made by means of a cheque requisition form.

There are many forms of payment method apart from cash and cheques. These include automated payment through computer links.

Payments are recorded in the cash book. The cash book may have analysis columns to remind us what the payment was for and to make posting to the main ledger more straight forward.

Discounts are not strictly a cash book transaction but are shown there as a memorandum to explain why some payments have been made for less than the invoice.

'Totals' figures should be checked for accuracy.

Cash book entries are posted to the main ledger accounts, the subsidiary accounts and discounts allowed accounts where appropriate.

The Purchases Ledger Control account is regularly reconciled to the Purchases Ledger to ensure accuracy of the figures.

Amounts both owing and due to the same customer may be set-off by a contra entry.

Practice Questions

Chapter 8

8.1

You have the following statement from Barton Supplies

STATEMENT OF ACCOUNT

BARTON SUPPLIES

21 Springfield Close, Immingham, IM21 3FY

To

Dawson Supplies
45 Scartho St
Immingham
IM15 2BH

Account SL 32

Date 6th March 2015

Date	Details	Debit £	Credit £	Balance £
02/02/2015	Balance b/f	760.90		760.90
06/02/2015	Chq received		744.65	16.25
06/02/2015	Disc allowed		16.25	0.00
09/02/2015	Inv 5298	176.25		176.25
16/02/2015	Inv 5420	528.75		705.00
23/02/2015	Inv 5550	352.50		1057.50
25/02/2015	Credit Note CN259		58.75	998.75

TOTAL AMOUNT OUTSTANDING **998.75**

All the invoices and credit note have been authorised for payment. You are told that you are entitled to a cash discount of £24.96.

Complete the remittance advice and cheque on the next page. Today's date is 9th March 2015 and the cheque will be signed by the Finance Director later.

Dawson Supplies

45 Scartho Street, Immingham, IM15 2BH

Remittance advice

Supplier: Barton Supplies

Date	Transaction ref	Amount (£)

CHEQUE TOTAL [ ]

IMMINGHAM BANK plc 30 - 25 - 81

14 Springfield Road, Brigg, DN20 3GF

Date ____________

Pay ____________ A/C Payee

£ [ ]

Cheque number 001481 | Sort Code 30-25-81 | Account number 12560798 | S Craggs

CHAPTER 8
Making Payments

8.2

What method of payment would be most appropriate for the following:

1. The electricity bill which is received at the company premises every 3 months. A Direct Debit is not used
2. Paying the sales representative for travel and accommodation while he/she is away on business
3. Purchase of a new premises for £350,000. The transfer of the money is required the same day
4. Paying wages to the 50 staff
5. The managing director's new company car.

8.3

The following is a list of payments made by your company for the week commencing 2nd March 2015.

2nd March	Paid J Austin, a creditor, £293.75. Cheque no 567259
2nd March	Paid B Barber, one of our sales team, £65.00 travelling expenses (no VAT). Cheque no 567260
3rd March	Paid rent, £250.00. Cheque no 567261
4th March	Paid K Slater, a creditor, £572.81. A discount of £12.50 was taken. Cheque no 567262
4th March	Made a cash purchase of £96.00 (inc VAT). Cheque no 567263
5th March	Bought stationery for £66.00 (inc VAT). Cheque no 567264
5th March	Paid L Doyle, a creditor, £556.04. A discount of £11.87 was taken. Cheque no 567265.
6th March	Paid wages of £250 (no VAT). Cheque no 567266

Show the entries in the cash book (payments side). Total the columns and post the amounts to the appropriate accounts.

CASHBOOK - PAYMENTS CBP83

Date	Detail	Discount Received		Bank		Cash Purchases		VAT		Purchases Ledger		Other Expenses	
		£	p	£	p	£	p	£	p	£	p	£	p

PURCHASES LEDGER

Dr			J Austin Account		Cr
Date	Details	£	Date	Details	£

Dr			K Slater Account		Cr
Date	Details	£	Date	Details	£

CHAPTER 8
Making Payments

Dr		L Doyle Account			Cr
Date	Details	£	Date	Details	£

MAIN LEDGER

Dr		Purchases			Cr
Date	Details	£	Date	Details	£

Dr		Other expenses			Cr
Date	Details	£	Date	Details	£

Dr		VAT Account			Cr
Date	Details	£	Date	Details	£

Dr		Purchases Ledger Control Account			Cr
Date	Details	£	Date	Details	£

Dr		Discounts Received Account			Cr
Date	Details	£	Date	Details	£

CHAPTER 8
Making Payments

8.4

You have the following opening balances on 1st April 2015.

Main ledger

Purchases	£5,600.00 Debit Balance
Purchases Returns	£150.00 Credit Balance
VAT	£460.00 Debit Balance
Purchase Ledger Control	£1095.00 Credit Balance

Subsidiary Purchases Ledger

H Nelson	£390.00 Credit balance
J Cook	£425.00 Credit balance
F Drake	£280.00 Credit Balance

The following transactions took place in the first week in April 2015

1st April	Bought goods on credit from H Nelson for £200.00 + VAT (invoice 2359)
2nd April	Bought goods on credit from F Drake for £350.00 + VAT (invoice 7963)
2nd April	Returned goods worth £50 + VAT to J Cook because they were faulty (credit note CN59)
3rd April	Bought goods on credit from J Cook worth £100 + VAT (invoice 432)
4th April	Bought goods on credit from H Nelson worth £250.00 + VAT (invoice 2368)
4th April	J Cook has a debit balance in the subsidiary sales ledger of £175.00. It has been agreed to set this off against the outstanding balance in the purchases ledger

Enter the opening balances in the relevant accounts

Enter the transactions above in the purchases day book and the purchases returns day book and total the columns

Record the transactions in the appropriate accounts (including the set off)

Balance off all accounts

Reconcile the purchases ledger control account with the subsidiary accounts

PURCHASES DAY BOOK **PDB 87**

Date	Invoice	Customer	Total		Purchases		Other expenses		VAT	
			£	p	£	p	£	p	£	p
		TOTAL								

PURCHASES RETURNS DAY BOOK **PRDB 05**

Date	Cr Note	Customer	Total		Purchases returns		Other returns		VAT	
			£	p	£	p	£	p	£	p
		TOTAL								

CHAPTER 8
Making Payments

MAIN LEDGER

Dr			**Purchases**		Cr
Date	Details	£	Date	Details	£

Dr			**Purchases Returns**		Cr
Date	Details	£	Date	Details	£

Dr			**VAT Account**		Cr
Date	Details	£	Date	Details	£

Dr			**Purchases Ledger Control Account**		Cr
Date	Details	£	Date	Details	£

PURCHASES LEDGER

Dr			**H Nelson Account**		Cr
Date	Details	£	Date	Details	£

Dr		J Cook Account			Cr
Date	Details	£	Date	Details	£

Dr		F Drake Account			Cr
Date	Details	£	Date	Details	£

Reconciliation of Purchases Ledger Control Account
4th April 2015

	£	£
H Nelson		
J Cook		
F Drake	______	
TOTAL		
TOTAL PER PURCHASES LEDGER CONTROL		
Discrepancy (if any)	nil	

Chapter 9

Petty Cash

In this chapter we will be looking at the Petty Cash Book
We shall see how to make a claim from the Petty Cash
We will look at recording payments from the Petty Cash Book
We will see how money is kept for the Petty Cash payments
We shall see how to balance the Petty Cash Book.

Recording all cash transactions in the cash book can make the cash book unmanageable as a record of payments made. Particularly in larger businesses, many small transactions take place daily, from buying stationery, stamps, tea and coffee, and paying the window cleaner. If these were all recorded in the cash book then it would make it difficult to see all the substantial payments. For this reason many companies have a small amount of cash kept on hand by a business for incidental expenses. This small amount of cash is called the **Petty Cash**.

'Petty' here does **not** mean 'unimportant'. It comes from the French word 'petit' meaning 'small'. 'Cash' returns to its original meaning of notes and coins. Expenses paid out of the petty cash are not paid by cheque.

Procedures and controls are vital as it can be the main area where money goes missing in an organisation. As little cash as is necessary should be kept on the premises so hundreds of pounds should not be kept as petty cash if only tens of pounds are spent each week.

Petty cash is usually kept in a petty cash tin, which is a lockable tin which has restricted access. Usually only one person has the authority to pay out any money. When not in use the petty cash tin will be kept in a locked drawer or cabinet or may even be kept in a safe. The money should be kept separate from any other money on the premises, particularly cash income. An upper limit on claims from the petty cash is usually enforced. Amounts above this figure should be made via a cheque requisition.

Money in the petty cash tin should have been withdrawn from the bank. It should not be topped up from cash receipts. Expenses should not be paid out of cash receipts, but should always go through the petty cash.

CHAPTER 9
Petty Cash

Let us suppose that your manager has asked you to go to the Post Office to post a parcel and while you are there you should pick up some envelopes. You go to the Post Office and buy the items, but you must remember to get and keep a receipt. On your return you take the receipt to the Petty Cashier who will complete a **Petty Cash Voucher.** This must be completed before Petty Cashier can give you the money out of the tin.

Petty Cash vouchers

The main form of control for petty cash is the use of petty cash vouchers. A petty cash voucher is completed for each item of expenditure.

Petty Cash Voucher No 0369

Date prepared *25/11/14*

Expenditure	Amount (£)
Envelopes	*3.40*
Postage	*0.75*
VAT	*0.68*
TOTAL	£ *4.83*

Paid to P Green

Authorised *R Skipworth*

Petty cash vouchers are numbered sequentially. This is a control to ensure that all cash is accounted for. If a mistake is made then the voucher should be kept and marked as void.

The date must be written on the voucher.

What the expenditure is for should be written along with the amounts for each item. VAT can be calculated and shown separately to make it easier when it comes to recording the voucher (see later in this chapter).

The total payment should be entered to show what amount has been paid out of petty cash.

There should be two signatures; the person to whom the cash has been paid, and (most importantly) the signature of the person authorising the payment.

The voucher should be accompanied by relevant documentation such as a receipt. The receipt may not show the amount of VAT particularly if it is for a small amount. You may even have to establish if VAT has been charged at all. You will see if the supplier is VAT registered as there must be a VAT registration number on the receipt if he/she is.

However, certain items do not attract VAT. You will learn more about these items in the Indirect Tax unit at level 3, but for now the most common ones which don't have VAT are;

Food and drink (but not meals prepared in a restaurant or takeaway)
Books and newspapers
Postage (if supplied by the Post Office)
Transport (but not taxis and private hire cars)

In the voucher shown on the previous page, the VAT is for the envelopes but not the postage.

EXAM ALERT!

A favourite question in exams is to calculate the VAT and net amount from the gross amount. Make sure you are completely comfortable with the method as described on p 37 of this book.

Before the petty cashier pays out of the petty cash he/she must be sure that the claim is valid. All expenses must be for business purposes. In some cases it will be left to company policy to decide which expenses are valid claims.

Tea and coffee is usually agreed by the company as a valid expense. Travel between home and work is a private expense unless it is a special call out. Occasionally people who work unsocial hours may claim for a taxi home if, for example, it's in the early hours of the morning and other forms of public transport are not available at that time. As a general rule, however, travel from home to work is not a valid expense to the business. If the petty cashier is unsure then he/she should take advice. Claims for fuel for a car must be carefully examined to ensure that the expense was for the business and not for private use. (HMRC will allow a flat rate of 45p per mile for tax purposes, so this would be a guide as to how much is reasonable to pay. This figure is correct at the time of going to press but may change. You should check the current rate with HMRC).

It is also usual to put a limit on each claim. Up to £25 for any one claim is usual although other amounts are used. Amounts above this should be referred to a supervisor and possibly an expense claim form completed.

The Imprest method

The most common method of operating a petty cash system is the **Imprest method**. This works on the basis that you only replace the amount you have spent. So if your petty cash starts the week with £100.00 in the tin (the imprest amount) and during the week you spend £90.00 then the top up for the beginning of the next week will be £90.00. This will mean that every week you will start with £100.00 and also, during the week, the amount of notes and coins plus the value of all the vouchers will come back to the imprest amount.

A non-imprest system is where the cash is topped up as and when the petty cashier thinks he needs to or it maybe that a set amount is put into the cash tin each week. This method is more difficult to control as there is no incentive to ensure that all money paid has been documented, and no one is really sure how much money should be in the tin at any one time.

The petty cash book

Just as we have a cash book, so we have a **petty cash book**. The petty cash book will be completed from the petty cash vouchers.

Petty Cash Book															
Receipts		Date	Detail	Voucher Number	Total		Analysis Columns								
							VAT		Postage		Admin		Cleaning		
£	p				£	p	£	p	£	p	£	p	£	p	

CHAPTER 9
Petty Cash

The layout is slightly different to what we have seen in other accounts. The 'Date' column and the 'Details' column are used for both receipts and payments.

The receipts column is on the far left. Usually the only amounts entered in this column is the balance b/d after it has been balanced (see later in this chapter) and the amount of top up received from the bank (or the cashier in larger organisations).

The 'Voucher Number' column refers to the petty cash voucher number.

The 'Total' column is the total amount paid for the goods or services.

Basically that is all that needs to be in a petty cash book, with receipts on the left and payments on the right. However, most petty cash books will have analysis columns (similar to the analysis columns in the cash book). The example above shows a small number of these analysis columns. Each of these columns will usually have a corresponding account in the main ledger. The analysis column makes it much easier to post expenses to the main ledger.

Balancing the petty cash book

Let us now have a look at a typical petty cash book which has all the entries for the week. You will note that the stamps don't have VAT as they are exempt and the window cleaner is obviously not registered for VAT. Had there been a 'stationery' column, the envelopes would probably be shown in this column, but the number of columns has been limited here for clarity of the principles. You should remember that how the expense is analysed is up to the business – there are no hard and fast rules.

Petty Cash Book															PCB17
Receipts		Date	Detail	Voucher Number	Total		Analysis Columns								
							VAT		Postage		Admin		Cleaning		
£	p	2014			£	p	£	P	£	p	£	p	£	p
50	00	3rd Nov	Balance b/d											
		3rd Nov	Stamps	45	3	60			3	60				
		4th Nov	Window cleaner	46	20	00							20	00
		5th Nov	Photocopy paper	47	12	00	2	00			10	00		
		6th Nov	Calculator	48	7	14	1	19			5	95		
		7th Nov	Envelopes	49	5	40	0	90	4	50				

At the end of the week we will need to top up the petty cash. We add up all the payments and this is the amount we need to put back into the petty cash. (£3.60 + £20.00 + £12.00 + £7.14 + £5.40 =) £48.14. Notice how this amount is debited to the petty cash book as it is money going into the account.

Petty Cash Book															PCB17
Receipts		Date	Detail	Voucher Number	Total		Analysis Columns								
							VAT		Postage		Admin		Cleaning		
£	p	2014			£	p	£	P	£	p	£	p	£	p	
50	00	3rd Nov	Balance b/d												
		3rd Nov	Stamps	45	3	60			3	60					
		4th Nov	Window cleaner	46	20	00							20	00	
		5th Nov	Photocopy paper	47	12	00	2	00			10	00			
		6th Nov	Calculator	48	7	14	1	19			5	95			
		7th Nov	Envelopes	49	5	40	0	90	4	50					
48	14	7th Nov	Cash received												

Now we need to balance it.

Add up both columns. The receipts column comes to £98.14 and the payments column is £48.14. The difference is the amount to carry down of £50.00.

Enter the £50.00 balancing amount in the payments column. Now both sides balance at £98.14. This amount should be entered in each side in a similar way to when we balanced ordinary accounts. However, this time we need the totals of the analysis columns. If you add these totals together and add the balance b/d you should come to the total balance figure. £4.09 + £8.10 + £15.95 + £20.00 + £50.00 = £98.14.

Finally we bring down the balance ready for the start of the new week.

You will notice that the amount of top up was the amount that was spent out of petty cash during the week. This shows the imprest system. Of course a different amount of top up would be required if the system was non-imprest.

Petty Cash Book														PCB17
Receipts		Date	Detail	Voucher Number	Total		Analysis Columns							
							VAT		Postage		Admin		Cleaning	
£	p	2014			£	p	£	P	£	p	£	p	£	p
50	00	3rd Nov	Balance b/d											
		3rd Nov	Stamps	45	3	60			3	60				
		4th Nov	Window cleaner	46	20	00							20	00
		5th Nov	Photocopy paper	47	12	00	2	00			10	00		
		6th Nov	Calculator	48	7	14	1	19			5	95		
		7th Nov	Envelopes	49	5	40	0	90	4	50				
48	14	7th Nov	Cash received											
		7th Nov	**Balance c/d**		**50**	**00**								
98	**14**				**98**	**14**	4	09	8	10	15	95	20	00
50	**00**	**10th Nov**	**Balance b/d**											

LEARNING POINT

Make sure you know how to manually balance a petty cash book. Computerised cash books may not balance the petty cash book so that it looks like this, but you will be expected to know how to do it the manual way.

Posting the petty cash book figures

We haven't quite finished yet. Remember that by entering the figures in the petty cash book we've only done half of the double entry. For the payments we'll need to update the relative expense accounts and the VAT account (if we are registered for VAT).

MAIN LEDGER

Dr		Postage Account			Cr
Date	Details	£	Date	Details	£
07/11/14	PCB 17	8.10			

Dr		Administration Account			Cr
Date	Details	£	Date	Details	£
07/11/14	PCB 17	15.95			

Dr		Cleaning Account			Cr
Date	Details	£	Date	Details	£
07/11/14	PCB 17	20.00			

Dr		VAT Account			Cr
Date	Details	£	Date	Details	£
07/11/14	PCB 17	4.09			

Don't forget that the cash book will need to show a credit entry for payment of the top up.

CHAPTER 9
Petty Cash

Petty cash control account

We have so far used the example that the petty cash book is used as part of the double entry. Some companies prefer to keep their petty cash book separate from the main ledger. There are two main reasons why a company may wish to do this:

1. There may be many entries in the petty cash book which will 'clutter' the main ledger accounts
2. Errors in the petty cash book postings will only come to light when the **Trial Balance** is drawn up, often only at the end of the year. (We will look at the Trial Balance in detail later in this book. For now you need to know that the Trial Balance is used to help us draw up a Profit & Loss for the year and a Balance Sheet). This could cause delays in producing our annual accounts.

Where the petty cash book is not used as part of the double entry, a **petty cash control account** is needed. The advantage of this is that the control account and petty cash book can be checked (reconciled) at regular intervals so that any errors can be found maybe weekly rather than only at the year end.

A petty cash control account for the petty cash in the example above would look like this:

Dr	**Petty Cash Control Account**				Cr
Date	Details	£	Date	Details	£
03/11/14	Balance b/d	50.00	07/11/14	PCB 17	48.14
07/11/14	Cash Book	48.14	07/11/14	Balance c/d	50.00
		98.14			98.14
10/11/14	Balance b/d	50.00			

Notice the debit entry for £48.14 for the top up which would also show as a credit entry in the cash book. The credit entry of £48.14 would balance with the total entries into the expense accounts.

Chapter Summary

Payment of small amounts for day to day expenses are paid out of petty cash.

Petty cash is notes and coins usually kept in a lockable tin with an authorised person to issue money from it.

When money is paid out of the petty cash a receipt will be required and a petty cash voucher is made up.

The most common system of keeping petty cash is the imprest method.

Payments are recorded in a petty cash book.

The petty cash is topped up at regular intervals from the bank and recorded as a receipt in the petty cash book and a payment in the cash book.

The petty cash book is balanced at regular intervals, usually at the same time as the top up.

Figures from the petty cash book are posted to the main ledger expense accounts.

A petty cash control account may be used if the petty cash book itself is not part of the double entry.

CHAPTER 9
Petty Cash

Practice Questions

Chapter 9

9.1

One of your tasks is to keep the petty cash. You can authorise payments up to £25 for each claim. Today's date is 9th April 2015 You have the following claims:

A Begum has an invoice for postage stamps he was asked to buy for the office. The invoice is for £3.60 (no VAT)

T Simpson has bought a new Laser Toner cartridge. The receipt is for £48.00 (including VAT)

C Murphy has a taxi fare receipt for a trip to a customer on business. The receipt is for £6.00 (including VAT)

S Marshall's car broke down and so had to get a taxi to work. The receipt is for £7.80 (including VAT)

K Ali has been to buy tea and coffee for the office. It is agreed that this is a genuine business expense. The receipt is for £8.75 (no VAT)

You are to prepare petty cash vouchers for each **valid** claim. Use the Petty Cash vouchers on the next page.

9.2

The petty cash is kept using the imprest method. The petty cash starts each week with £50.00. The following is a list of the petty cash vouchers authorised during the week.

April 13th 2015	Voucher Nº 157	Taxi fare £7.00 (including VAT)
April 13th 2015	Voucher Nº 158	Photocopy Paper £20.40 (including VAT)
April 14th 2015	Voucher Nº 159	Parcel postage £0.75 (no VAT)
April 15th 2015	Voucher Nº 160	Highlighter pens £2.40 (including VAT)
April 16th 2015	Voucher Nº 161	Envelopes £5.40 (including VAT)
April 17th 2015	Voucher Nº 162	Train fare £10.50 (no VAT)

You are to complete the petty cash book.
Bring down a balance at the start of the week.
Enter the vouchers and complete the analysis columns.
Top up the petty cash and bring down a balance ready for the beginning of the next week.
Total the columns.
Use the Petty Cash Book on p167.

Petty Cash Voucher **No 0465**

Date prepared

Expenditure	**Amount (£)**
VAT	
TOTAL	**£**

Paid to ______________

Authorised ______________

Petty Cash Voucher **No 0466**

Date prepared

Expenditure	**Amount (£)**
VAT	
TOTAL	**£**

Paid to ______________

Authorised ______________

Petty Cash Voucher **No 0467**

Date prepared

Expenditure	**Amount (£)**
VAT	
TOTAL	**£**

Paid to ______________

Authorised ______________

Petty Cash Voucher **No 0468**

Date prepared

Expenditure	**Amount (£)**
VAT	
TOTAL	**£**

Paid to ______________

Authorised ______________

Petty Cash Book														PCB21
Receipts		Date	Detail	Voucher Number	Total		Analysis Columns							
							VAT		Travel		Stationery		Postage	
£	p				£	p	£	p	£	p	£	p	£	p
			Balance b/d											
			Balance c/d											
			Balance b/d											

(This page is left blank for your notes)

Chapter 10

Wages and Salaries

> In this chapter we will be looking at Payroll.
>
> We shall look briefly at how wages and salaries are calculated
>
> We shall look at what deductions are made from gross pay
>
> We will see how payments are made to employees
>
> We will look at how wage payments are recorded in the double entry system.

Payroll is not covered by the AAT. If you want to study in depth how to run a payroll then you should consider one of the payroll courses offered by Premier Training.

However, in this unit you will be expected to know the basics of how wages are paid, what deductions from gross wages must and may be made, and how to record these payments.

Payroll is defined as a list of employees receiving salaries or wages, and the amounts due to each. The amounts due to each employee is called a wage or a salary.

A salary is usually an amount paid to an employee as specified in his/her contract. It is usually an annual amount which is paid in instalments periodically (typically monthly). A wage on the other hand is where each job, unit of production, or hour is paid separately. The remuneration is typically weekly. For example a salary may be £20,000 per year, but a wage may be £9.61 per hour or £384 per week. While all these amount roughly to the same payment, they are expressed in a different way.

The amount you earn is called **gross pay**. This is not the amount you receive as there are several statutory deductions which we shall see in a moment. The amount you actually receive is called **net pay**.

Gross pay can be made up of several amounts. First there is the **basic pay**. This is the amount as agreed in the contract of employment. Someone who earns a salary may be given one twelfth of the annual amount each month as basic pay. Someone who earns (say) £10.00 per hour will get £400 if they work 40 hours in the week.

Another type of gross pay is **overtime**. Usually this is paid for extra hours worked over and above those stated in the contract. Most workers have the right not to work for more than 48 hours per week on average (although they can elect to do so). Most overtime is paid at a premium. This means that they are paid an extra amount above the regular rate. So overtime may be paid at 'time and a half', which means that an employee who is generally paid £10.00 per hour will be paid £10.00 basic for extra hours plus an extra half (£5.00 per hour). Some employees are paid overtime for working unsocial hours (for example on a Sunday, a bank holiday, or through the night).

Gross wages may be increased by a **bonus**. A bonus is often given to employees for particularly good work. It may be offered as a reward or an incentive.

Commission can be paid on the basis of amounts sold and received by the company. It is most commonly used for salespeople. So if a particular salesperson makes £1,000 worth of sales, the commission may be 10% of the sales (i.e. £100). Some workers may work on a commission basis only, meaning that the commission is their only gross pay.

Piece work is paid on the basis of units produced or action performed. So if a factory worker makes 100 units in a week at a rate of £4.00 per unit then he/she will be paid £400 for the week. Workers paid on this basis may either be paid entirely on the piece rate, or as an extra amount over and above their basic pay.

Before an employee receives any pay entitled to him/her, there will be deductions made by the employer. These fall into two categories

Statutory deductions
Voluntary deductions

Some payments are required by law. For example if you are off sick or if you are on maternity leave. There are strict rules on when you can be paid these and how much you are entitled to. How to calculate these are covered in other courses offered by Premier Training. For now you just need to know that employees may be entitled to these.

The **Statutory Deductions** are those which are required by law. These include **Income Tax**, **National Insurance** and **Student Loans**. These are all paid to Her Majesty's Revenue and Customs (HMRC).

Income Tax is the tax levied by the government on amounts earned. Everyone (including children and pensioners) are subject to income tax. The reason that most children and pensioners do not actually pay income tax is because there is a free allowance (called the **personal allowance**) and these groups of people may not earn above this tax free amount. This amount changes each year. For the 2013/14 tax year it is £9,440. People over 65 may be entitled to a higher allowance. This amount may be adjusted by Her Majesty's Revenue and Customs (HMRC) so the correct amount of tax is collected if the employee receives benefits such as a company car, or if there are arrears of tax still owing, or if the employee has income from another source. It may also be adjusted for allowances such as a special work clothes allowance. This tax free allowance is spread evenly through the year into 12 or 52 equal amounts, depending on the frequency of pay. In this way income tax will be paid at a relatively even rate each week or month. Any amounts above the free allowance is **taxable pay** and will be taxed at a certain rate. For the 2013/14 tax year it is 20%. Those who earn more than £32,010 above the free

allowance will pay tax at 40% on the excess pay. Those who earn over £150,000 above the free allowance will pay tax at 50% on the excess.

You pay **National Insurance** contributions (NICs) to build up your entitlement to certain social security benefits, including the State Pension. The type and level of NIC you pay depends on how much you earn and whether you're employed or self employed. The amount you pay will also depend on whether you contribute to certain types of company pension. You don't pay NICs until you reach the age of 16 and you stop paying NICs when you reach State Retirement age. There are many rates of NICs depending on an employee's circumstances but typically you will pay 12% on income between £149 and £797 per week. Employers are also charged National Insurance for all the employees they have. Again this will vary with circumstances, but typically an employer will pay 13.8% on the wages above £148 per week.

Student Loans are loans offered to students while in Higher Education. They have to be paid off when a person reaches a certain level of income. What level of income will depend on what kind of loan it was. The most recent students (since 1998) will pay 9% of everything they earn above £16,365 until the debt is paid off.

The employer may also be instructed to take regular amounts from pay by a court or a council (known as **attachment of earnings** or AOEs). This may be for Maintenance Payments, Arrears of Council Tax or other such amounts owed.

If you are an employee, Income Tax, National Insurance and Student Loans will be collected by your employer and paid to HMRC (Her Majesty's Revenue and Customs). This is called **PAYE** (Pay As You Earn). It is a legal requirement that employers **must** collect statutory deductions from wages and pay the amounts to HMRC.

Voluntary Deductions are not required by law, but the employer will usually take off these agreed amounts before you actually get your pay. The employer may take agreed amounts from your pay for:

Pension Contributions (The employer often makes payments to the employees pension also)
Charitable donations
Regular savings schemes
Union Fees

These are just the most common voluntary deductions. Others are possible.

CHAPTER 10
Wages and Salaries

LEARNING POINT

The rates and thresholds shown here are correct at the time of going to press. However, taxation changes at regular intervals, typically annually. While you won't need to know the rates and thresholds in this unit, you can check on the latest ones at http://www.hmrc.gov.uk/payerti/forms-updates/rates-thresholds.htm

Payslips

Every employee is required by law to be given a free itemised payslip. There is no set format, but they must show:

Employer Name
Employee name
Gross pay
How the gross pay is made up
A breakdown of all deductions
The total of all deductions
The net pay as paid to the employee

A typical payslip is shown on the next page.

CROCKETT ASSOCIATES

PAYSLIP

Employee Name	A Dawson	Pay Date	30.6.2014
Employee Number	10000282	Tax Period	03
NI Number	AB123654C	Tax ref	673/U1
Tax Code	944L		

Payments		Deductions	
Description	Amount	Description	Amount
Basic	1666.00	Tax	258.60
Overtime	250.00	Employee NI	157.68
		Union	20.00
Total Payments	**1916.00**	**Total Deductions**	**436.28**
	Gross Pay	Tax	EE's NIC
This period	1916.00	258.60	157.68
Year to date	5248.00	675.60	413.52
		NET PAY	**1479.72**

Payment of wages

Cash

Since the passing of the Wages Act 1986, employees can no longer insist on payment in cash. However, any employee paid in cash before this Act cannot be compelled to change to cheque or credit transfer. So it is now less and less common for wages to be paid in cash, and it is more cost effective for businesses to pay by other means.

Those employers who still pay in cash will need security measures when cash is on the premises ready for payment. Normally the amount due to each employee is calculated and then the number of notes and coins required is worked out. This is important as you must be able to give each employee exactly the amount due. It is no good getting to the last employee and find you don't have the right notes and coins to pay him/her exactly to the penny.

Some companies have a special form to calculate what notes and coins are required. It is called a cash analysis. There is an example below. Normal practice is that the required number of notes and coins is telephoned through to the bank so this can be prepared in advance of collection. This saves time both for the bank and for your company.

Cash analysis

Week ....13.......

	£50	£20	£10	£5	£2	£1	50p	20p	10p	5p	2p	1p	TOTAL
A O'Brien	1	2	1		3				1	1		1	106.16
J Francis	1	1	1		1	1	1		1	1	2		83.69
K Rees		2	1	1	1			1	1		2		57.34
C Grant	2	2			1		1			1	1	1	142.58
D Hart	1	1		1		1		1			1	1	76.23
Number	5	8	3	2	6	2	2	2	3	3	6	3	
Total (£p)	250.00	160.00	30.00	10.00	12.00	2.00	1.00	0.40	0.30	0.15	0.12	0.03	466.00

When paying wages by cash, security is of great importance. Procedures may include having two people collecting the money from the bank, or you may even hire a security firm who will collect it for you. When it is returned to the office to be made up into the wage packets the office should be locked and entry should be restricted.

A slip showing the number of notes and coins should be included in the wage packet and each employee should sign for the wage packet as they receive it. Employees should be asked to check the contents immediately and they should be made aware that mistakes cannot be rectified once the employee has left the area of the office. Wages should only be given to the employee personally. You should never ask someone to pass on wages.

Cheque

It is more common to pay wages by cheque. This avoids the problems of security with cash and also saves time by not having to count out notes and coins. Cheques can be written out by hand or some payroll computer packages will print out the cheque and the payslip at the same time.

Obviously there are some security measures which need to be adopted with cheques. The cheques themselves need to be stored in a secure place, preferably a safe. The cheques should never be pre-signed. Some companies require two signatures (or more) on a cheque and the person signing the cheque should check the amount matches the net amount on the payslip.

BACS

By far the most common method of paying wages is by BACS (see also p89 and 90). Over 90% of the UK workforce is paid in this way. The organisation will need to give each employee's bank details to its own bank. Then when payday approaches a list of all employees and the amounts to pay are given to the organisation's bank (Day 1). On Day 2 the information is passed to the employee's bank and processed. On Day 3 the money is simultaneously credited to the employees' account and debited from the organisation's account. Employees who leave and new employees can be updated on the bank files simply on amendment forms provided by the bank.

As you can see, the whole process is a lot more secure, requiring no more security measures than ensuring that the information is kept secret. The chances of theft are removed completely. Of course the amount of payment will still need to be checked and authorised before the information is passed to the bank.

Payment to HMRC

As shown above, an employer has a legal requirement to deduct statutory deductions from employees' wages and pay these amounts to HMRC. The payment is usually made monthly and is due on the 22nd of each month following the month of payment. So deductions made in September will be due for payment by 22nd October.

Payment in almost all cases is now required to be made electronically. However, if payments are made by cheque the due date is the 19th of the following month.

Double entry accounting of wages and salaries

Wages are an expense to an organisation, but what the organisation pays is not the same as what the employee receives. The expense to the organisation will be made up of payments to the employee, payments to HMRC and payments to other organisations under the employee's voluntary deductions. Typical accounts to use are

Cash book
Wages account (expense account)
HMRC account
Pension account

A Wages Control account is usually used. We have dealt with Sales Ledger Control accounts and Purchases Ledger Control accounts earlier in this book. The control account is still a summary of all the other transactions, but here it is used as a check that all relevant transactions have been posted. It also allows the various entries to be made at different times. Without it all the entries would have to be made at the same time.

Let us assume that for the month

Gross pay	£25,000
Net pay (i.e. payment received by the employees)	£17,614
Income tax deducted	£4091
National Insurance Contribution (employee)	£2045
National Insurance Contribution (employer)	£2500
Pension contribution (employee)	£1250
Pension contribution (employer)	£1250

(Over the coming years the employer will be required by law to contribute towards the employees pension fund).

We will start with the gross pay

Dr		Wages Expense Account			Cr
Date	Details	£	Date	Details	£
30/11/14	**Wages Control**	**25,000**			

Dr		Wages Control Account			Cr
Date	Details	£	Date	Details	£
			30/11/14	**Wages Exp**	**25,000**

We have debited the expense account with the gross wages and recorded this entry in the control account.

This is not the only expense to the company. You will remember that the organisation will also need to pay employer National Insurance contributions and (in this case) employer pension contributions.

Dr		Wages Expense Account			Cr
Date	Details	£	Date	Details	£
30/11/14	Wages Control	25,000			
30/11/14	**Employer NICs**	**2,500**			
30/11/14	**Emp'er Pension**	**1,250**			

Dr		Wages Control Account			Cr
Date	Details	£	Date	Details	£
			30/11/14	Wages Exp	25,000
			30/11/14	**Employer NICs**	**2,500**
			30/11/14	**Emp'er Pension**	**1,250**

(Note how the other side of the double entry is **always** in the wages control account).

You will notice how employer NICs and Employer pension contributions are an extra expense to the organisation over and above the basic wage cost.

Now let's pay our employees. Here I've used a 'Bank account' for simplicity. It could just as well be shown in the cash book if the cash book is used as part of the double entry.

Dr		Wages Control Account			Cr
Date	Details	£	Date	Details	£
30/11/14	**Bank**	**17,614**	30/11/14	Wages Exp	25,000
			30/11/14	Employer NICs	2,500
			30/11/14	Emp'er Pension	1,250

Dr		Bank Account			Cr
Date	Details	£	Date	Details	£
			30/11/14	**Net Wages**	**17,614**

Now we can show what we owe to HMRC

Dr		Wages Control Account			Cr
Date	Details	£	Date	Details	£
30/11/14	Bank	17,614	30/11/14	Wages Exp	25,000
30/11/14	**PAYE**	**4,091**	30/11/14	Employer NICs	2,500
30/11/14	**NICs Emp'ee**	**2,045**	30/11/14	Emp'er Pension	1,250
30/11/14	**NICs Emp'er**	**2,500**			

Dr		HMRC Account			Cr
Date	Details	£	Date	Details	£
			30/11/14	**PAYE**	**4,091**
			30/11/14	**NICs Emp'ee**	**2,045**
			30/11/14	**NICs Emp'er**	**2,500**

Finally let's show what we owe to the pension provider

Dr		Wages Control Account			Cr
Date	Details	£	Date	Details	£
30/11/14	Bank	17,614	30/11/14	Wages Exp	25,000
30/11/14	PAYE	4,091	30/11/14	Employer NICs	2,500
30/11/14	NICs Emp'ee	2,045	30/11/14	Emp'er Pension	1,250
30/11/14	NICs Emp'er	2,500			
30/11/14	**Pension Emp'ee**	**1,250**			
30/11/14	**Pension Emp'er**	**1,250**			

Dr		Pension Fund Account			Cr
Date	Details	£	Date	Details	£
			30/11/14	**Pension Emp'ee**	**1,250**
			30/11/14	**Pension Emp'er**	**1,250**

Notice how the entries for Employer NICs and Employer Pensions appear on both sides of the Wages Control account.

Let us now balance the Wages Control Account

Dr		Wages Control Account			Cr
Date	Details	£	Date	Details	£
30/11/14	Bank	17,614	30/11/14	Wages Exp	25,000
30/11/14	PAYE	4,091	30/11/14	Employer NICs	2,500
30/11/14	NICs Emp'ee	2,045	30/11/14	Emp'er Pension	1,250
30/11/14	NICs Emp'er	2,500			
30/11/14	Pension Emp'ee	1,250			
30/11/14	Pension Emp'er	1,250			
		28,750			**28,750**

You can see that this account balances to zero. If this happens then you can be almost certain that all the required postings have been made.

When it comes to paying the Tax and National Insurance by the 22nd of the next month the double entry is to debit the HMRC account and credit the Bank account (or cash book). Similar entries will be made when you pay the pension fund.

EXAM ALERT!

While it is unlikely that you will have to post all the entries to all the accounts from memory, you should be aware of the principles and know what is shown in each account.

Marks are often lost because students have forgotten to add the employer NICs in the relevant accounts, particularly on both sides of the Wages Control account.

You should also be careful when asked which account to update. Remember to identify the account and not what the figure represents.

Chapter Summary

Gross pay is the amount an employee earns; net pay is the amount the employee takes home.

There are two types of deduction an employer makes from gross pay; statutory deductions and voluntary deductions.

Statutory deductions include Income Tax and National Insurance Contributions.

Voluntary deductions may include payments to a pension or Union subscription.

Employees may be paid in cash, by cheque or by BACS.

The employer is legally responsible for deducting tax and national insurance and paying it to HMRC.

The payment of wages is recorded in the double entry accounting system.

The correct postings can be confirmed by the use of a Wages Control Account.

CHAPTER 10
Wages and Salaries

Practice Questions

Chapter 10

10.1

You have the following payroll totals for the month of April 2015.

Gross Pay	£16,800
Income Tax deducted	£2,816
NIC Employee Contribution	£1,024
NIC Employer Contribution	£1,638
Pension Employee Contribution	£800
Pension Employer Contribution	£800

a) Calculate the total wages cost to the employer

b) Calculate the amount to be paid to HMRC

c) Calculate the amounts to be paid to the pension fund

d) Complete the double entry for wages in the main ledger accounts

Dr		Wages Expense Account			Cr
Date	Details	£	Date	Details	£

Dr		Wages Control Account			Cr
Date	Details	£	Date	Details	£

CHAPTER 10
Wages and Salaries

Dr		Bank Account			Cr
Date	Details	£	Date	Details	£

Dr		HMRC Account			Cr
Date	Details	£	Date	Details	£

Dr		Pension Fund Account			Cr
Date	Details	£	Date	Details	£

10.2

a) In the above accounts what do the credit entries in the HMRC Account represent?

b) In the above accounts what do the credit entries in the Pension Fund Account represent?

c) What is the latest that these amounts should these amounts be paid?

Chapter 11

Methods of Communication

> In this chapter we will see the need for effective communication.
>
> We shall look at the various means of written communication.
>
> We shall look at various formats of written communication.
>
> We will see how businesses have their own unique identity through written communication.

To be effective in business you have to be a good communicator. As an Accounting Technician you may well have to communicate effectively with customers and suppliers as well as people in your own organisation.

First and foremost is the need to be polite. Being polite does not necessarily mean giving in to what the other person wants. Indeed, you may need to chase late payment from customers, which will need firmness as well as politeness. Being polite in itself will not always win your case, but by not being polite you will almost certainly not get your way or win your argument.

The greatest skill in effective communication is to see things from the other person's point of view. If you always say what **you** want and how **you** want to do things then you will make no progress in effective communication. While you should not let the other person control matters, you should always be receptive to their point of view and be ready to accept alternative ideas to achieve the goal you require. The only person you can be sure of changing is you, so if you can adapt what is required or how it is done to suit the other person, as long as it achieves the required goal, you are well on the way to promoting better relationships.

Most people tend to focus on what is wrong. Of course, you need to be clear on what the problem is, but you also need to be clear on what works well. So if you have a problem with a customer who is late paying his/her invoice, you need to say that, but you should also say how the problem can be resolved. Compare the following narratives:

"It is now over 2 months since we sent you Invoice No 12345. You haven't paid it yet and we need you to pay it immediately"

"We note from our records that Invoice No 12345 is still outstanding. Since it was sent over 2 months ago, it is now considerably overdue. We would appreciate settlement by return of post as per your usual method of payment."

The second example is more likely to get a result than the first as you have stated the problem but avoided confrontation. There is also the solution to the problem. Of course if this doesn't get a result then you may have to be a little more firm, but this should be the kind of language you use in a first request letter.

You must be clear about what you mean and what your intention is. If you are not then other people can misinterpret what you mean (sometimes deliberately if it is to their advantage).

Don't make unconfirmed assumptions. For example, don't assume that someone hasn't paid their invoice because they hope to avoid paying it (even if you think this is what has happened). Assumptions aren't all bad as long as you state what they are. It is quite alright to say *"I assume the goods you bought arrived in good condition"*, and may lead to the reason for the request for payment.

Avoid conflict at all costs. Conflict rarely gets satisfactory results. State your case and accept the other person's point of view (even if you think it may be a lame excuse). *"I sent the cheque in the post last week"* should **not** be answered by *"well why haven't we got it?"*. This is confrontational. You should accept their response but suggest how the problem can be resolved, in this case, either by tracing the cheque by its number or issuing a new one. If they are telling the truth then the problem can be resolved easily; if they're bluffing they won't be able to tell you the cheque number and will have to issue a new one anyway.

The way you respond also has a massive effect on the way you and your company are perceived. Being polite, efficient, firm, yet responsive will get you more customers than if you are not.

Business communication should never be 'chatty'. Usually business people don't have time for the niceties of unimportant information. While you should ensure that your communication covers all the required points and gives sufficient data, you shouldn't write two pages where two lines would do. Being succinct is an essential skill in business.

The Note

The simplest and most basic form of written communication in any organisation is the note. It is used as a quick and easy method of conveying messages between people, usually in the same or neighbouring offices or departments. Because it is quick and simple it is usually hand written.

A note should include:

The name of the person it is from
The name of the person it is to
The time and date the note was written
A clearly stated message

An example note is shown below:

To: *J Murray*

Date: *24th November 2014*

Time: *2.15pm*

Mr Watts called from Asco Ltd. He wants to set a time for a meeting with you.

Please call back on 01752 627398 before 5.30pm

T Rose

Memorandum

A memo or memorandum is a type of communication commonly used in businesses. Memos are sent to colleagues and co-workers. They are less formal than a letter, but more formal than a note. They do not require a salutation ('yours faithfully' or 'yours sincerely') or a closure statement as in business letters or even a signature or name at the bottom.

A memo is used as a written reminder or to convey a short proposal or some basic information. They are usually short and to the point. An example is given on the following page.

Memorandum

To: M Hughes

cc: R Crockett

From: A Dawson

Date: 24th November 2014

Re: December Sales Forecast

Please can you supply me with your forecast for sales for next month by the end of the week.

I need the information for a meeting on 1st December.

Thank you

You will notice that the 'to' and 'from' are at the top along with a 'cc'. 'Cc' stands for 'carbon copy' and it tells you that a copy of the memo has gone to this person. ('Bcc' is also possible with electronic memos. It stands for 'blind carbon copy' whereby the recipient is not made aware that a copy has been sent to anyone else).

The sender's name is put at the top along with the date and a short title explaining the subject matter of the memo.

If other material such as documents or tables are enclosed these are listed at the end after you have put 'encl'. This ensures that the recipient is aware of the extra material and can see what should be there.

Memoranda (the plural of memorandum) can be hand written or word processed. Memoranda are often the most common form of written communication within a business and can be sent by email between departments or sites.

CHAPTER 11

Methods of Communication

Fax

Fax is the abbreviated form of facsimile. It is a system for the electronic transmission of images over telephone lines. Since it copies anything, both pictures and words can be sent by this means. Advertising material as well as letters and documents are sent between fax machines, and as long as you have the fax number (which will be similar to a telephone number) faxes can be sent anywhere in the world.

A fax header sheet is usually sent at the beginning of the fax to show:

Who it is to
Who it is from
The fax number and phone number
The number of pages sent
The date
What the fax is about
The names of anyone on copy

Fax

To:	L Lowe	**From:**	Dawson Supplies
Fax:	01469 585444	**Pages:**	2 including this header
Phone:	01469 585448	**Date:**	24th November 2014
Re:	Copy Invoice	**CC:**	C Berry

☐ **Urgent** ☐ **For Review** ☐ **Please Comment** ☐ **Please Reply** ☐ **Please Recycle**

CHAPTER 11
Methods of Communication

The Email

Email is short for 'electronic mail'. It is an electronic document (usually a message) sent from a computer to a person or group on the Internet or computers connected by a network. It can be used to send messages to a single person or a group of people. As with the memo, a 'cc' or 'bcc' can be used (see p186).

When you open an email account you will be given (or you can choose) an email address. Email addresses come in two parts. The part before the @ sign is the local part, which is often the user name of the recipient. The part after the @ sign is the host name where the email will be sent before it is downloaded (collected). (@ is pronounced 'at'). The domain is often the email provider such as 'hotmail' for Microsoft or 'Gmail' for Google. Alternatively it can be the name of the organisation that the recipient represents. The domain may also show the type of recipient (.com is a commercial organisation; .co is a company; although both these are used for individuals as there is no term for private addresses). Other examples are .org usually for non-profit making organisations and charities. Educational institutions use .edu while government uses .gov. The country of the domain is often added. Great Britain uses .uk while the United States uses .us and South Africa will use .za. A full email address could look like this:

jsmith@sample.co.uk

Email addresses are usually all lower case letters (small letters as opposed to capital letters). If upper case letters (capital letters) are used then it may be sent to a different address.

Received emails are stored at the domain address until they are downloaded (often automatically when the recipient logs in). A list of emails received will be shown and they can be opened individually.

Email was originally designed to send simple text messages, but now technology has allowed colours and pictures to be sent in the message. Be careful with colours and pictures in emails as over-use can look unprofessional.

Documents can be attached to emails although most mail servers will restrict the size of files that can be attached.

Below is an example of an email ready to be typed.

You will see the 'to' box, where the recipient's email address should be typed and the 'cc' box if anyone else is to receive the email. Emails can be sent to more than one address by putting a comma between the addresses. All emails should have a 'subject'. This is a title describing the contents of the email and will be shown in the recipient's received list before it is opened. An attachment box will appear if there are documents attached showing the file name of whatever is being sent with the email. Email is usually free and is almost instantaneous.

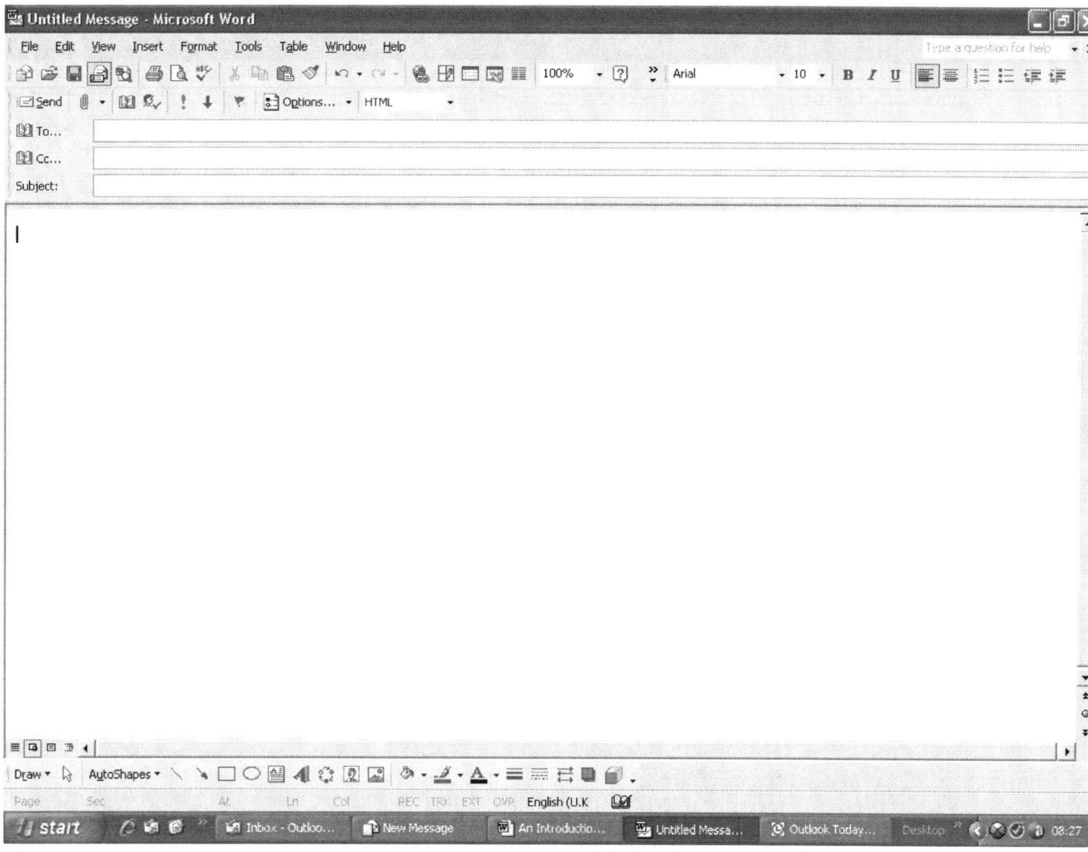

WARNING!

Opening an unsolicited email can cause unwanted downloads, especially of viruses, malware and adware. Some of these are programs designed to cause damage to the computer, while others cause advertising ‘pop-ups’ to appear while you are using other applications. Spyware are programs designed to monitor the users behaviour and can also collect personal and confidential information from the computer. These can also be downloaded from an email without the user’s knowledge.

All computers should have an anti-virus program installed. While it will not guarantee the computer won’t get infected, it will dramatically reduce the risk. However, even with an anti-virus program installed you should never open emails from unknown sources.

A growing problem with emails is *spam*. Spam is also known as "bulk e-mail" or "junk e-mail". It involves nearly identical messages sent to numerous recipients and often involves some kind of advertising. The real problem with spam is the sheer volume. As at August 2010 there were over 200 billion spam emails per day. While most of the emails are harmless in themselves, the problem comes when the recipients inbox becomes overloaded with spam. Some email inboxes may have over 100 spam items a day. Having to sort out the proper emails from the spam can be a time consuming (and annoying) task. Email addresses are collected from chat rooms and web sites and addresses may be sold to other 'spammers'. The amount of spam has been much reduced by better *filtering*. Filtering is where incoming emails are selected or rejected either by the sender's email address or by rejecting certain words in the title or content of the email. Filters are set up by the mail providers and can be adapted by the user if required.

Emails can be kept by the sender and the recipient on their computer almost indefinitely. This is useful if you wish to refer to the email in the future, but you may be subject to a limit by the provider or your organisation as these take up space in your computer's (or network's) memory. It is useful to check your old emails from time to time and delete unwanted items.

Business Letters

A business letter is a formal communication. To create the desired effect on the reader it is important to follow the following guidelines:

The letter should be in the correct format
It should be short and to the point
It should be relevant
It should have no grammatical errors or spelling errors
It should be polite (even if it's to complain or demand something)
It should be neat and well presented.

The next page shows a typical business letter.

The key elements are:

Often the company name or logo (but not essential)
Your address in the top right. (You could also include a telephone number and/or and email address here)
The name (if possible) and address of who you are writing to goes below this on the left
The position of the date is flexible but it usually goes below the addressee details
The salutation at the beginning depends on whether you have the person's name. If you have then it should be 'Dear Mr Patel' or Dear Mrs O'Neil. If you don't know the marital status of a woman then you should put Ms. If you don't know the name of the person then you should put 'Dear Sir or Madam'.

A heading is useful particularly if you are referring to something in the main text. This goes directly below the salutation.

If you are replying to a letter which has a reference number then you should repeat this number. Often this is just above the date.

The content of your letter should be as short as possible, divided into short, clear paragraphs.

End the letter with 'Yours sincerely' if you have named the recipient. Use 'Yours faithfully' if you've started with 'Dear Sir or Madam'.

Sign your name and then print it directly below. If you are signing the letter in some capacity (e.g. Finance Administrator) then you should say so.

If there are documents enclosed then say so by putting 'Encl'. You may want to state what they are.

DAWSON SUPPLIES

45 Scartho Street,
Immingham,
IM15 2BH

Purchasing Department
Patel Fabrics
132 Anglian Way,
Norwich,
NR3 6FG

1st December 2014

Dear Sir or Madam:

Invoice 123456

We note from our records that we have not yet received payment of invoice 123456 for £1650.00. Our terms are strictly 30 days and so this amount is due immediately.

I am enclosing a statement of account.

Yours faithfully

Mr Alan Dawson
Finance Manager

Encl. Statement of account

CHAPTER 11
Methods of Communication

A person in business may well receive many letters each day. If your letter is 6 sides of thick text then it may well end up in the bin. Letters should take seconds to read. As a result get straight to the point. Use straight forward language and don't use long words just for the sake of it. Don't repeat too much information which is on an enclosed document. The reader is quite capable of reading the document him/herself.

Spelling mistakes and bad grammar often give a bad impression of your company. If you are using a word processor then use the spell checker. Check the spelling yourself anyway as the spell check will not pick up all the errors (cf. 'their' and 'there').

Check the grammar. Some word processing packages will do this for you, but if not make sure you have written in complete sentences and check the punctuation. If you're not sure then you should get someone else to look at it.

Use the right tone of language. Avoid slang or colloquial language. It's better to say a company has gone into liquidation than the company has 'gone bust'. Avoid contractions ('it's', 'I'm') and don't use vague words such as 'nice' or 'get'. Don't use emotive words or subjective language ('rubbish' or 'great').

Always be polite even if you're complaining and avoid too many long words and cliché phrases.

Make sure the letter is well presented. If it's hand written it should be neat and legible. Makes sure it's signed and dated and that you've spelt people's names correctly. Don't send a letter with coffee stains on it!

Many companies have a 'house style' letter. This is a uniform style of letter which will identify the company. House styles vary in complexity but will usually show the name, address and other details of the company and maybe the company's logo. All letters sent by the company will show this information in the same way.

House style letters may be printed stationery and extend to letters, faxes and memos as well as business cards and advertising material. Computers may store a template for letters and other stationery.

The Report

Reports are formal documents. They usually show the result of an investigation or finding. They have various styles, but in general they should include the following:

A title, which will include who the report is by and a date
An introduction which will briefly state the purpose of the report
The methods used in the report or where the information comes from
The results of your report
A conclusion

Each section should have at least a new paragraph. Most reports will contain subheadings such as 'Introduction', 'Method', 'Results' or 'Findings', and 'Conclusion'. Longer reports will have numbered paragraphs. Whatever the layout, a report must follow logically from one section to another. The conclusions should be made from the findings or data contained in the body of the report.

Chapter Summary

Effective communication is an important part of any business.

There are several forms of written communication:

A note

A memorandum (memo)

A fax (facsimile)

An email

A letter

A report

Each of these has its own format and its own style of English.

Many of these have their own 'house style' which uniquely identifies the company.

Computer 'house styles' are kept as a template.

CHAPTER 11
Methods of Communication

Practice Questions

Chapter 11

11.1

a) On an email what is the meaning of Cc and Bcc?

b) You need to send a copy of an invoice to your customer in the United States. What would be the quickest method of doing this?

11.2

You work at Dawson Supplies. Your manager comes to you saying that he has had a serious complaint from the buyer at T&T (Mr A Singh). Mr Singh has complained that although he ordered 20 rolls of fabric over a month ago he still hasn't received the goods. T&T is a valued customer and needs to be kept happy.

You check the records and find that the Purchase Order was received two days ago and delivery usually takes 1 week.

Your manager asks you to write a letter to Mr Singh at T&T. T&T's address is 154 Margaret St, Immingham, IM17 9RQ. Today's date is 1st May 2015. Show your response using the headed paper below.

DAWSON SUPPLIES	**45 Scartho Street,** **Immingham,** **IM15 2BH**

Chapter 12

Less Common Transactions

In this chapter we will review and explain the types of account kept in an accounting system.

We shall look at transactions in less frequently used accounts.

We shall see how a VAT account records payments due from or payments due to HMRC.

We shall see what bad debt is and how to record it in our accounts.

We shall see what a fixed asset is and the difference between capital expenditure and revenue expenditure.

So far we have looked at various types of account 'kept' in various ledgers.

Subsidiary Sales Ledger

This is where we keep all our customer accounts. Each account will show how much each customer owes us. Goods taken on credit will be recorded here as well as payments received for the goods. Goods returned and settlement discounts are also recorded here. Remember that an increase in what the customer owes is a debit entry and a decrease is a credit entry. Invoices raised for goods taken on credit will be a debit entry, whereas goods returned, settlement discounts taken, and payments received all reduce what is owed and should be credit entries.

LEARNING POINT

Cash sales are **not** recorded in the Sales Ledger. If a customer pay cash then he/she will not owe anything. As the Sales Ledger is where we record what is owed to us, cash sales are not part of this ledger. We probably won't know the name of the customer who pays cash anyway.

Don't confuse a cash sale with a payment from a customer who is paying his/her invoice. When the customer pays his/her invoice he/she is reducing the debt and so it must be recorded in the Sales Ledger.

The Subsidiary Sales Ledger serves to assist or supplement the Main Ledger so there is no double entry in any subsidiary account. The double entry in the Main Ledger which records what is owed to us is called the Sales Ledger Control account, which is a summary of the Subsidiary Sales Ledger.

LEARNING POINT

Don't confuse the 'Sales' account, the 'Sales Ledger' and the 'Sales Ledger Control' account. Each is quite a separate account or group of accounts. You must know what each account is for and when to make entries in them.

Subsidiary Purchases Ledger

This is where we keep all our supplier accounts. Each account will show how much we owe each supplier. Goods taken on credit will be recorded here as well as payments made for the goods. Goods returned and settlement discounts are also recorded here. Remember that an increase in what we owe the supplier is a credit entry and a decrease is a debit entry. Invoices received for goods taken on credit will be a credit entry, whereas goods returned, settlement discounts taken, and payments made all reduce what we owe and should be debit entries.

You should notice that the entries here are a mirror image of those in the Subsidiary Sales Ledger. Invoices are on the other side of the account and payments are also on the other side.

Again, cash purchases are not recorded here. The Subsidiary Purchases Ledger records what we owe to whom. If we pay cash we don't owe anything.

LEARNING POINT

Cash purchases are **not** recorded in the Purchases Ledger. If we pay cash then we will not owe anything. As the Purchases Ledger is where we record what we owe, cash sales are not part of this ledger.

Don't confuse a cash purchase with a payment to a supplier when we are paying our invoice. When we pay our invoice we are reducing the debt and so it must be recorded in the Purchases Ledger.

Since the Subsidiary Purchases Ledger is *subsidiary* then there is no double entry. The double entry in the Main Ledger which records what we owe is called the Purchases Ledger Control account, which is a summary of the Subsidiary Purchases Ledger.

CHAPTER 12
Less Common Transactions

> **LEARNING POINT**
>
> Don't confuse the 'Purchases' account, the 'Purchases Ledger' and the 'Purchases Ledger Control' account. Each is quite a separate account or group of accounts. You must know what each account is for and when to make entries in them.

Cash Books

These books are where the money in and money out is recorded. There are two types of cash book mainly used:

The cash book
The petty cash book

The cash book is the main book where the cash finances of the company are recorded. It will record all transactions to and from the bank and possibly also record what cash amounts are being held on the premises. (Often, if cash is banked every day, then what cash is on the premises will not be recorded; just what has gone into and what has come out of the bank).

The cash book may also analyse the payments and receipts so that each transaction can be categorised.

The cash book may record any settlement discounts taken either by the customer or by us. Strictly speaking this is not a cash book entry as it does not involve the movement of cash, but may be shown here to help explain why amounts paid or received do not match exactly what is owed.

The cash book often doubles as a book of prime entry **and** part of the double entry. Alternatively the cash book may be used simply as a book of prime entry with the main ledger account being a 'bank' account and possibly a 'cash' account.

The petty cash book records payments of small value. This helps free up the cash book from too much clutter. The petty cash book will analyse the payments so payments can be categorised. As the amount in petty cash will be topped up at regular intervals so there will be regular entries from the cash book to the petty cash book to show this top up.

As with the cash book, the petty cash book may double as a book of prime entry and part of the double entry, or alternatively it will simply be used as a book of prime entry with the main ledger account being the 'petty cash control account'. (Remember that 'control' in these accounts means 'summary').

CHAPTER 12
Less Common Transactions

Main Ledger

The Main Ledger is where the double entry system takes place. It can be split into two types of account.

Nominal accounts
Real accounts

A nominal account is where expenses, losses, income and gains are recorded. Sales and purchases come into this category as well as any bank loans and the VAT account. A 'Capital' account also come under this heading. A Capital account records the amount of money invested by the owner in the business. There will also be a 'drawings' account. Owners of businesses do not get wages or a salary; they get *drawings*.

Real accounts are those usually relating to tangible (touchable) aspects of the business. So a company's computers, cars and other goods used in the business all are recorded in real accounts. Stock of goods, the bank account (you can touch the money) and the petty cash control account are all real accounts as are the sales and purchases control accounts.

Accounts which are less frequently used

Expense accounts

We have looked briefly at some expense accounts. Expense accounts will include rent, electricity, car running expenses, wages, telephone, etc. All should show a debit balance. This fits in with our concept of a debit being the 'receiving' as we get benefit from all of the expenses so we receive it, even if this is rent or wages. The double entry for paying our rent should be:

Debit Rent account
Credit Cash book (or bank account)

Sometimes we get credit for an expense. For example we may get an electricity bill which we don't have to pay until the end of the month. The double entry for receiving the bill is:

Debit Electricity
Credit Creditor account (in this case the electricity company)

Some companies like to keep their purchases ledger (and purchases ledger control) separate for regular purchases of goods for resale and for purchases of other goods and services. In these cases a Sundry Creditor Ledger and a Sundry Creditor Control account will be kept separate from the Purchase Ledger and Purchase Ledger Control.

When payment is made to the electricity company the double entry will be:

Debit Creditor account
Credit Cash book (or bank account)

Income accounts

Some businesses will have income from other sources other than normal trading. The most common example of this is when a company has spare space in its buildings and rents this space out.

To record such income in the books is similar to an expense account but on the other side

Debit Cash book (or bank account)
Credit Rent received (or whatever the type of income)

Of course, if you send out invoices for this type of income you may have to raise a non-trade debtors account

Debit Non-trade debtors
Credit Rent received

Loans accounts

Most businesses will have a loan from the bank. This will need to be recorded in the accounts with a loan account. When the loan is taken out and the amount is put in the bank, the double entry will be:

Debit Cash book (or bank account)
Credit Loan account

The loan is a liability to the company and all liabilities are credits. In our 'giving' and 'receiving', the liability is the amount we are due to give so it is a credit

When we repay all of part of the loan the entries will be the other way round

Debit Loan account
Credit Cash book

It's not usually as simple as that though as many loans are paid back in amounts which contain an element of the capital repayment and an element of interest. The interest due is an expense, whereas the capital repayment isn't. In these cases you will need to split the repayment into its two parts and record each in its own account:

Debit Loan account
Debit Interest charged
Credit Cash book

CHAPTER 12
Less Common Transactions

Stock account (Inventory Account)

Stock valuations are carried out at least once a year. Some businesses value stock monthly, weekly or occasionally daily. However, stock accounts are usually only altered by a physical stock check.

The double entry required to record the valuation of stock will require accounts called a *'Trading, and Profit & Loss account'*. Trading, and Profit & Loss accounts will be covered in more detail later in your studies. For now you will just need to know that there are two accounts where amounts are transferred in order to calculate and record what profit or loss has been made by the company in a particular period. There is the **Trading account** and the **Profit & Loss account**. (Profit & Loss is often shortened to P&L).

So the stock valuation will be recorded as:

Debit Stock
Credit Trading account

Stock is an asset which is something from which we *receive* benefit and so it is a debit.

Capital account

Capital accounts are where the owner of a business records the amount of money he/she has put into the business. All commercial businesses need an input of money to start trading. Stock will need to be bought before it is sold. Premises will need to be bought or rented and shop fittings will need to be purchases.

For the purposes of accounting, the owner of a business is looked on as being quite separate from the business itself. All the transactions are regarded as being undertaken by the business rather than the owner. Therefore, whatever money the owner has put into the business is owed back to the owner which is a liability to the business. For this reason, a capital account will always have a credit balance, as it is money which is due to be *given* back to the owner.

So when the owner opens up his/her business by putting money into the business bank account the entries will be:

Debit Cash book (or bank account)
Credit Capital account

Of course the owner may not just put money into the business; he/she may put their own vehicle or property into the business. The double entry for taking the owner's vehicle into the business would be:

Debit Vehicle account
Credit Capital account

CHAPTER 12
Less Common Transactions

Drawings account

Owners of businesses don't get paid wages. They do need to take money out of the business though. After all that is why they set up in business in the first place. Money (and goods) taken by the owner for his/her own use are called drawings. It is necessary to see how much has been taken in a 'drawings' account. The double entry for cash drawings would be:

Debit Drawings
Credit Cash book (or bank account)

If the drawings are taken in goods then the account to credit will be the purchases account (not the stock account as this is only changed by a stock count at the end of the period). If the goods are taken by the owner then the goods cease to be 'purchases' as they are no longer intended for resale (see p113). The double entry would then be:

Debit Drawings
Credit Purchases

At the end of the year the drawings account will be credited and the capital account will be debited to record the fact that the business does not owe so much back to the owner. The capital account will be reduced by the amount of drawings

Fixed Assets (Non Current Assets)

Fixed assets normally include items such as land and buildings, motor vehicles, furniture, office equipment, computers, fixtures and fittings, and plant and machinery. It is really anything which is brought into the business which will be used over a number of years. A separate account will be needed for each type of fixed asset such as 'motor vehicles account', 'buildings account' or 'machinery account'.

The double entry for the purchases of a fixed asset is:

Debit Motor Vehicles (or whatever the fixed asset is)
Credit Cash book (or bank account)

Of course if the fixed asset is bought on credit then the cash book will be replaced by a sundry creditor account.

Bad Debt account

A debt goes bad when it becomes apparent that the debt will never be paid. This is one of the risks of giving credit to customers. Of course, there will usually be a policy to try to recover overdue debts, but when phone calls, letters, and even possibly legal action have all failed then the expense has to be born by the company. Legal action should not be undertaken where the cost of recovery is more than the debt itself. So if legal action costs amount to £100 and the debt is for £20 then obviously the company would not proceed. The expense will be written off to a bad debt account. The double entry to write off a debt is:

Debit	Bad Debts written off
Credit	Sales Ledger control (remembering to also credit the individual customer account)

You will remember that in most cases VAT is accounted for when the sale is made (see chapters 2 and 3). If you have raised a VAT invoice then you owe HMRC the amount of VAT you have charged, whether or not you have actually received payment or not. You can see then that if a customer does not pay then you may have already paid the VAT. In effect you will have paid the VAT on your own sale.

Because of this, HMRC will allow relief on bad debts. As long as the debt is more than 6 months overdue and it is written off in your own books then you can reclaim the VAT. You should note that the debt must be 6 months **overdue** and not just 6 months old. So if you raise an invoice on 1st January and offer 30 days credit then it is due for payment on 31st January. Only 6 months after 31st January are you able to claim back the VAT you paid (i.e. 31st July).

The double entry to write off a bad debt which includes an element of VAT would be:

Debit	Bad Debts written off (the net amount)
Debit	VAT account (the VAT amount)
Credit	Sales Ledger Control (the full amount including VAT)

VAT account

Let us look more closely at the VAT account. You have already seen how to record VAT on sales and purchases in the VAT account in earlier chapters. Let us look again at what can go in a VAT account

Dr			**VAT Account**		Cr
Date	Details	£	Date	Details	£
VAT on Purchases			VAT on Sales		
VAT on the purchase of Fixed Assets			VAT charged on other income		
VAT on expenses			VAT on Purchase Returns		
VAT on Sales Returns					
VAT on relief for bad debts					

You can probably see that when you balance this account (see p63) you could have either a debit balance or a credit balance. A credit balance shows how much you owe to HMRC. (Payment of VAT is usually made every 3 months). A debit balance on the other hand shows that HMRC will give you a refund of VAT. If this is the case you should expect a refund at the end of the 3 month period.

Let's look at an example

Dr		VAT Account			Cr
Date	Details	£	Date	Details	£
Oct 2014	VAT on Purchases	5,000	Oct 2014	VAT on Sales	6,500
Oct 2014	VAT on expenses	200	Oct 2014	Rented out van	50
Nov 2014	VAT on Purchases	5,550	Nov 2014	VAT on Sales	6,000
Nov 2014	VAT on expenses	150	Nov 2014	Purchase return	100
Nov 2014	Sales return VAT	50	Dec 2014	VAT on Sales	8,000
Dec 2014	VAT on Purchases	7,000			
Dec 2014	VAT on expenses	400			
Dec 2014	Fixed Asset Purchase	3,000			
Dec 2014	Bad debt relief	200			

So now let's balance the account

Dr		VAT Account			Cr
Date	Details	£	Date	Details	£
Oct 2014	VAT on Purchases	5,000	Oct 2014	VAT on Sales	6,500
Oct 2014	VAT on expenses	200	Oct 2014	Rented out van	50
Nov 2014	VAT on Purchases	5,550	Nov 2014	VAT on Sales	6,000
Nov 2014	VAT on expenses	150	Nov 2014	Purchase return	100
Nov 2014	Sales return VAT	50	Dec 2014	VAT on Sales	8,000
Dec 2014	VAT on Purchases	7,000	**Dec 2014**	**Balance c/d**	**900**
Dec 2014	VAT on expenses	400			
Dec 2014	Fixed Asset Purchase	3,000			
Dec 2014	Bad debt relief	200			
		21,550			**21,550**
Jan 2014	**Balance b/d**	**900**			

You can see that in this case a repayment is due from HMRC of £900. When you receive it you would:

Debit Cash book (or bank account)
Credit VAT account

This means that the VAT account would now be zero, which is as it should be as no one owes anything until another sale or purchase is made. However, in real situations the VAT account never balances to zero because sales and purchases are being made all the time and it is unlikely you will receive payment before you make another sale or purchase.

Revenue and Capital expenditure

It is important to make the distinction between capital and revenue expenditure so that a true reflection on the profitability of the company (or otherwise) can be correctly shown.

Let us take an example of a small business. At set up of the business the owner may purchase new premises for £350,000. The business makes total sales of £200,000 per year. You can probably see that although sales figures are good, the purchase of the property would lead to a substantial loss if the property were to be included in the profit and loss calculation.

Now let us come to the next year. Sales are not so good this year and only come to £50,000. The property was bought last year and so doesn't come into the figures this year. The company shows a profit this year albeit a very small one.

From this example you can see that the first year showed good sales but finished up with a substantial loss. Year two was quite a bad year but showed a profit. By taking into account the purchase of the property in the first year the profit and loss has not shown a true reflection of now the business in performing.

Therefore we must class the purchase of the property as **capital expenditure**. When we do this the total cost of the property will not be shown in the calculation of the profit and the profit calculation will show us more clearly how the business is doing. (In actual fact the cost of the property will be spread over a number of years in the form of depreciation, but calculations for this will be dealt with later in the course).

What can and can't be classed as capital expenditure has been the subject of much debate over the years. It may be clear that in the example above the purchase of the property will be classed as capital expenditure, but what about a new shop window that was installed in year 3, or the repair to the leaking roof in year 4? It is also a legal requirement to classify which is which as you are charged tax on your profits and profits are affected by revenue expenditure and not capital expenditure.

Although each type of expenditure will need to be assessed separately to establish if it is capital or revenue expenditure, there are a few basic guidelines.

CHAPTER 12
Less Common Transactions

Capital expenditure

Buying any fixed asset (see p201 for what a fixed asset is)
Expenditure bringing the new fixed asset into a state where it can be used in the business. This will include installation costs and fixing problems which existed before the purchase
Delivery costs of fixed assets
Improvements (but not repairs) of fixed assets (so you can classify a new shop window as capital expenditure if there wasn't a shop window there before, but not if it is simply to replace a broken one)
Legal costs in buying land or property

Revenue expenditure

Maintenance of fixed assets (including fuel for cars and vans, road fund licence and insurance, servicing of machines and cars)
The day to day running costs (including administration costs, wages, stationery, delivery expenses, selling and distribution expenses)

As a general guide, anything which will last for less than a year will also be a revenue expense.

You must also remember that what is capital expenditure to one company may not be capital expenditure to another. If you deal in computers and sell them as part of your trade then the purchase of a computer is not a capital expenditure. However, if you sell clothes (for example) and you buy a computer to help in your office then the computer **will** be a capital expenditure. It is the nature of what it will be used for which is important and not the nature of goods themselves.

Revenue and capital income follow the same idea. Revenue income is income from the sale of goods or services; capital income is income from the ownership of non-trading items. If a company sells a product to a customer and receives payment then this is revenue income, but if a company holds shares in another unattached company and receives a dividend then this will be capital income.

Chapter Summary

Accounts can be grouped into various ledgers:

1. Subsidiary Sales Ledger
2. Subsidiary Purchases ledger
3. Cash books
4. Main Ledger

There are accounts which are used less frequently:

1. Income and expenditure accounts
2. Loan accounts
3. Stock accounts
4. Capital and Drawings accounts
5. Fixed Asset accounts
6. Bad Debt accounts

The VAT account will show all transactions involving VAT and when balanced will show the amounts due to or from HMRC.

Expenses must be classified correctly into capital or revenue.

Practice Questions

Chapter 12

12.1

You business is registered for VAT. The following transactions took place

6th April 2015	Started business with £5,000 capital in the bank
6th April 2015	Bought office furniture for £2,000 + VAT
6th April 2015	Bought a computer for £800 + VAT (show in office equipment account)
13th April 2015	Paid rent £150 by cheque (No VAT)
13th April 2015	You receive payment for advertising space in your shop. £50 + VAT
13th April 2015	Your loan from the bank comes through for £4,000. (Shown in the bank loan account)
17th April 2015	Took £100 from the bank as drawings
20th April 2015	Receive payment for the advertising space. £50 + VAT
24th April 2015	Took drawings of £150 from the bank
27th April 2015	Receive payment for the advertising space. £50 + VAT
27th April 2015	Repay some of the loan. £100 (£33 interest; £67 capital repayment)

You are to enter the above transactions into the appropriate accounts shown below

CASH BOOK

RECEIPTS PAYMENTS

Date	Detail	Bank £	Date	Detail	Bank £

CHAPTER 12
Less Common Transactions

Dr			Capital Account		Cr
Date	Details	£	Date	Details	£

Dr			VAT Account		Cr
Date	Details	£	Date	Details	£

Dr			Office Furniture Account		Cr
Date	Details	£	Date	Details	£

Dr			Office Equipment Account		Cr
Date	Details	£	Date	Details	£

Dr			Rent Paid Account		Cr
Date	Details	£	Date	Details	£

Dr			Advertising Receivable Account		Cr
Date	Details	£	Date	Details	£

Dr		Bank Loan Account			Cr
Date	Details	£	Date	Details	£

Dr		Drawings Account			Cr
Date	Details	£	Date	Details	£

Dr		Interest Payable Account			Cr
Date	Details	£	Date	Details	£

12.2

Balance off the VAT account above and say whether the balance is an amount owing to or an amount owing from HMRC. The date is 30th April 2015

12.3

Our customer, G Lopez, has gone into liquidation. He owes us a total of £2,400 (including VAT). All the debts are over 6 months old so we can claim bad debt relief from HMRC. Show what debit entries and what credit entries are require to write off this bad debt. (Note that the company operates a Sales Ledger Control account)

12.4

Your company buys a new machine for the factory. Show which costs are capital and which are revenue

a) List price of the machine
b) The cost of having the machine delivered
c) Paying our own employees extra to install the machine
d) One year's maintenance cover

(This page is left blank for your notes)

Chapter 13

The Cash Book and Bank Statement

> In this chapter we shall look at how to check the cash book against the bank statement.
>
> We will see how to balance a cash book.
>
> We shall learn how to reconcile the bank statement to the cash book.

We have already seen how to post items to the cash book on both the receipts and payments sides. Now we will see how it is checked and balanced. This happens usually once a month to coincide with the date on the bank statement which is usually received every month.

The next page shows the cash book entries for September. For simplicity there is only a 'bank' column (i.e. no cash column) and the expenses column is limited to 'Other expenses'. In a real cash book it would be spread over two pages, with the left hand page for the receipts and the right hand page for payments. This leaves room for many more analysis columns as required. However many columns there are, the principle is the same.

You will see in the details of some of the payments, the cheque numbers. Remember that 'cash' payments can mean notes and coins, cheque or debit/credit card.

After the cash book, you will see the statement from the bank. (Note how the entries are on the other side to the cash book. Payments are on the left and receipts on the right. This is because the bank is showing things from its point of view.) You will notice that the opening balance in the cash book and the opening balance on the bank statement are different. The reason for this is that some entries posted to the cash book had not yet been recorded by the bank. Cheques may be recorded in the cash book as soon as they are sent, but the receiver can't get his/her money for 4 days, and in addition, he/she has 6 months to pay the cheque into his/her bank account. Cash and cheques paid into the bank late in the day on the last banking day of the month may not show on the statement until the first banking day of the next month.

In this case cash and cheques for £2365.00 paid into the bank must have been recorded in our cash book on the last working day of August, but they are not showing on the bank statement until the first banking day of September.

The cheque No 500102 has obviously been paid several days ago, but it is not showing on our bank statement until 5th September. We shall see in more detail how to do a **bank reconciliation** later in this chapter. For now we will need to be aware of late entries in the bank statement.

CASH BOOK

Date	Detail	Discount Allowed	Bank	Cash Sales	VAT	Sales Ledger	Date	Detail	Discount Received	Bank	Cash Purchases	VAT	Purchases Ledger	Other Exp
1/9/14	Balance b/d		950.75											
1/9/14	Cash Sales		480.00	400.00	80.00		2/9/14	Cash Purchase (500103)		600.00	500.00	100.00		
8/9/14	G Hall	10.00	223.25			223.25	10/9/14	M Ahmed (500104)	10.00	283.75			283.75	
15/9/14	K Khan		350.00			350.00	17/9/14	Rent (500105)		95.25				95.25
22/9/14	Cash Sales		600.00	500.00	100.00		22/9/14	C Kaur (500106)		534.96			534.96	
29/9/14	Cash Sales		120.00	100.00	20.00		30/9/14	Wages		525.50				525.50
							30/9/14	Cash Purchase (500107)		360.00	300.00	60.00		

THE BANK STATEMENT

IMMINGHAM BANK plc
14 Springfield Road, Brigg, DN20 3GF

STATEMENT

Account name: Dawson Supplies   Statement no: 133

Account number : 12560798   30-25-81

Date	Details	Payments £	Receipts £	Balance £
2014				
1st Sept	Balance brought forward			1,049.25 O/D
1st Sept	CC		2,365.00	1,315.75
5th Sept	500102	365.00		950.75
5th Sept	CC		480.00	1,430.75
6th Sept	500103	600.00		830.75
15th Sept	500104	283.75		547.00
19th Sept	CC		573.25	1,120.25
26th Sept	500106	534.96		585.29
26th Sept	CT: Fry Supplies		7,500.00	8,085.29
27th Sept	500105	95.25		7,990.04
27th Sept	CC		600.00	8,590.04
30th Sept	Cash Withdrawal	525.50		8,064.54
30th Sept	Bank Charges	57.39		8,007.15

CC: Cash and cheques   DD: Direct Debit

CT: Credit transfer   O/D Overdrawn

The next task is to match all the entries in the cash book and on the bank statement. A good idea is to tick all those that match as you go along. The payment of £480.00 into the bank is shown on both and then there are the two cheque receipts which are shown as one entry on the bank statement.

The next entry on the bank statement is not quite so obvious, but you will see that the next two receipts in the cash book add up to this figure, so it seems these two receipts were banked together at the same time.

Cheque 500106 is shown on the bank statement before cheque 500105. Obviously cheque 500106 has been banked by the recipient more promptly than 500105. (Remember that cheques written by the company must be written in order and will be recorded in the cash book in numerical order. These cheques will be shown on the bank statement in the order they have been received by the bank, which is not necessarily the same order.)

The Credit Transfer (CT) from Fry Supplies isn't showing in our cash book. The bank has received an automated payment form a customer, but we haven't recorded this in our cash book because we didn't know about it until now. We will leave this unticked for now and deal with it in a moment.

There are just two more entries we can match; the payment into the bank for £600.00 and the £525.50 taken for wages.

So now we can see that there are two entries on the bank statement not accounted for in the cash book. We need to update the cash book with these amounts.

CASH BOOK

Date	Detail	Discount Allowed	Bank	Cash Sales	VAT	Sales Ledger	Date	Detail	Discount Received	Bank	Cash Purchases	VAT	Purchases Ledger	Other Exp
1/9/14	Balance b/d		950.75											
1/9/14	Cash Sales		480.00	400.00	80.00		2/9/14	Cash Purchase (500103)		600.00	500.00	100.00		
8/9/14	G Hall	10.00	223.25			223.25	10/9/14	M Ahmed (500104)	10.00	283.75			283.75	
15/9/14	K Khan		350.00			350.00	17/9/14	Rent (500105)		95.25				95.25
22/9/14	Cash Sales		600.00	500.00	100.00		22/9/14	C Kaur (500106)		534.96			534.96	
29/9/14	Cash Sales		120.00	100.00	20.00		30/9/14	Wages		525.50				525.50
30/9/14	**Fry Supplies**		**7,500.00**			**7,500.00**	30/9/14	Cash Purchase (500107)		360.00	300.00	60.00		
							30/9/14	**Bank charge**		**57.39**				**57.39**

CHAPTER 13

The Cash Book and Bank Statement

The next task is to balance the cash book and total the analysis columns. The cash book should be balanced very much like any other account. Using the 'Bank' columns, the debits add up to £10224.00. The credit column comes to £2456.85, so we must add £7767.15 as the balance to carry down. The total for each column is then £10224.00 which should be entered as the total for each column. This figure must be the same figure as it is a check that you have entered the correct figures in the 'bank' columns, and you have the correct balance to carry down.

The analysis columns should then be totalled. If you add the credit side totals together they should come to the balance total **plus the balance c/d**. £800.00 + £160.00 + £818.71 + £678.14 + £7767.15 = £10224.00. Remember not to include the discounts column.

The debit side should be totalled and checked in the same way, but this time we have to add the opening balance. £1000.00 + £200.00 + £8073.25 + £950.75 = £10224.00

Finally the balance b/d will be entered into the opposite side to the balance c/d. This then tells us how much money we should have in the bank.

Of course, if the balance should appear on the other side of the cash book (i.e. a credit balance) then it means we are overdrawn. We have taken more money out of the bank than we have put in. If you have a cash column (and in the petty cash book) a credit balance is not possible as we can't have a negative amount of notes and coins.

CASH BOOK

Date	Detail	Discount Allowed	Bank	Cash Sales	VAT	Sales Ledger	Date	Detail	Discount Received	Bank	Cash Purchases	VAT	Purchases Ledger	Other Exp
1/9/14	Balance b/d		950.75											
1/9/14	Cash Sales		480.00	400.00	80.00		2/9/14	Cash Purchase (500103)		600.00	500.00	100.00		
8/9/14	G Hall	10.00	223.25			223.25	10/9/14	M Ahmed (500104)	10.00	283.75			283.75	
15/9/14	K Khan		350.00			350.00	17/9/14	Rent (500105)		95.25				95.25
22/9/14	Cash Sales		600.00	500.00	100.00		22/9/14	C Kaur (500106)		534.96			534.96	
29/9/14	Cash Sales		120.00	100.00	20.00		30/9/14	Wages		525.50				525.50
30/9/14	Fry Supplies		7,500.00			7,500.00	30/9/14	Cash Purchase (500107)		360.00	300.00	60.00		
							30/9/14	Bank charge		57.39				57.39
							30/9/14	**Balance c/d**		**7767.15**				
		10.00	**10224.00**	1000.00	230.00	8073.25			10.00	**10224.00**	800.00	160.00	818.71	678.14
1/10/14	**Balance b/d**		**7767.15**											

Bank reconciliation

You will now see that the bank statement and the cash book still don't balance, so every month we will need to do a **bank reconciliation statement** to explain the difference between the cash book and the bank statement.

You will need to follow company procedure on the layout of the reconciliation statement, but it's usual to start with the balance from the bank statement. You then need to take off any *unpresented cheques* (i.e. cheques you have written and sent as payment but which have not yet been banked by the recipient).

Then you will need to add *outstanding lodgements* (i.e. amounts you have paid into the bank but are not yet recorded on the statement).

Our bank reconciliation statement in the example above should look like this:

Bank Reconciliation Statement
30 September 2014

	£	£
Balance as per bank statement		8007.15
Less: unpresented cheques		
500107	360.00	
		7647.15
Add: outstanding lodgements		
	120.00	
Balance as per cash book		**7767.15**

So now we have a document that explains the difference between the bank statement and the cash book. This statement will be useful document. It is evidence that the cash book and bank statement were reconciled on a particular date, so future problems and errors don't need to go back further than this date. It will also be useful at the end of next month so we can check that the unpresented cheque and the outstanding lodgement have actually been recorded by the bank. In the case of outstanding cheques, if they are not showing on the bank statement they will need to be carried forward again.

EXAM ALERT!

You may have to reconcile a bank statement to a cash book. **Don't forget the opening balance**. Many marks have been lost in exams entering cheques into the cash book which suddenly appear on the bank statement. Remember that cheques are recorded in the cash book in sequence so you should not enter cheques with an earlier number. These will be shown on a previous page of the cash book and will be shown on the bank reconciliation at the end of the previous month. You are not always given these earlier documents.

Chapter Summary

The cash book needs to be checked against the bank statement every month.

The cash book must be updated with the missing entries shown on the bank statement.

The cash book must be totalled and balanced.

Remaining differences between the cash book and the bank statement must be shown in a bank reconciliation statement.

Practice Questions

Chapter 13

13.1

The following is your bank statement for May 2015

IMMINGHAM BANK plc
14 Springfield Road, Brigg, DN20 3GF

STATEMENT

Account name:	Dawson Supplies	Statement no:	141
Account number :	12560798		30-25-81

Date	Details	Payments £	Receipts £	Balance £
2015				
1st May	Balance brought forward			3502.72
4th May	CC		1,352.00	4,854.72
7th May	Chq 379652	741.00		4,113.72
8th May	Chq 379654	257.50		3,856.22
13th May	Chq 379656	1,251.27		2,604.95
15th May	Chq 379655	175.25		2,429.70
18th May	BACS Credit: P Green Ltd		2,475.00	4,904.70
25th May	Chq 379657	250.00		4,654.70
27th May	CC		1,279.56	5,934.26
29th May	Bank Charges	83.65		5,850.61

CC:	Cash and cheques	DD:	Direct Debit
CT:	Credit transfer	O/D	Overdrawn

The cash book shows the following transactions

CASH BOOK

RECEIPTS | PAYMENTS

Date	Detail	Bank		Date	Detail	Bank	
2015		£				£	
1st May	Balance b/d	3502	72	3rd May	G Evans Chq 379652	741	00
1st May	Cash deposit	1352	00	3rd May	H Edwards Chq 379653	421	65
27th May	Cash deposit	1279	56	3rd May	J Collins Chq 379654	257	50
29th May	Cash deposit	236	57	8th May	K Stewart Chq 379655	175	25
				8th May	L Sanchez Chq 379656	1251	27
				18th May	M Morris Chq 379657	250	00
				26th May	P Rogers Chq 379658	729	57

You are to

a) Check the items on the bank statement against the items in the cash book

b) Update the cash book as needed

c) Total the cash book and bring down a balance as at 1st June 2015

d) Prepare a bank reconciliation statement at 31st May 2015. Use the pro-forma on the next page.

Bank Reconciliation Statement
31 May 2015

	£	£
Balance as per bank statement		
Less: unpresented cheques		
Add: outstanding lodgements		
Balance as per cash book		

Chapter 14

Journals and the Trial Balance

In this chapter we shall look at why we use journals and how to prepare them.

We shall see the purpose of a Trial Balance and how to draw one up.

We shall look at what errors a Trial Balance will show and what errors it won't.

We shall look at how to correct errors found in the Trial Balance both temporarily and permanently.

In chapter 12 we saw how some accounts showed less common transactions. We saw how these transactions still required documentation (prime documents). Now we will look at the book of prime entry for such transactions.

A **journal** is not in itself part of the double entry system. Instead it records what entries should be made in the main ledger. A journal is a record of why some transactions have been put through the main ledger, and, because it records one transaction at a time, it reduces the risk of errors in the main double entry accounting system.

You don't use a journal for every transaction. A journal would not be used for regular items, such as the purchase of goods for sale. A journal provides a book of prime entry for less common transactions.

Let us look at a journal to record someone starting a business by putting £5,000 into a business bank account

Date	Details	Dr	Cr
2015		£	£
1st Jan	Bank account	5,000	
	Capital account		5,000
	Opening capital introduced		

Remember this is purely a record of what you will be doing in the main ledger.

CHAPTER 14
Journals and the Trial Balance

The essential parts of a journal are:

Date
Account(s) to be debited
Account(s) to be credited
The amounts to enter in each account. (The debits must always balance with the credits
A **narrative**. The narrative is an essential part of the journal as it explains why the entries have been made. If there is no narrative then it defeats the object of preparing a journal.

IMPORTANT POINT

Don't lose valuable marks by omitting the narrative on a journal. A journal is not complete without one.

Let's now look at something a little more complicated

Suppose that as well as opening a bank account, our new sole trader buys £1,000 worth of goods to sell and a van worth £8,000.

Date	Details	Dr	Cr
2015		£	£
1st Jan	Bank account	5,000	
	Purchases account	1,000	
	Vehicle account	8,000	
	Capital account		14,000
		14,000	14,000
	Opening assets introduced		

Here we can see that there are several accounts to debit with just one account to credit. Nevertheless the debit side still balances the credit side. We have shown this by totalling each side.

If we were to purchase some machinery on credit for £10,000 we would show this as follows. Here the company is registered for VAT and so the VAT can be recorded separately.

Date	Details	Dr	Cr
2015		£	£
1st Mar	Machinery account	10,000	
	VAT	2,000	
	Sundry Creditors account		12,000
		12,000	12,000
	Purchase of cutting machine on credit from Machine Cutters Ltd		

A trader may take drawings in a number of forms. There is simply taking cash from the bank for his/her own use. Alternatively the owner may take stock from the store. Another form of drawings is when part of the expense is for personal use. Take for example a phone bill. It may be estimated that one third of the phone bill is for private calls. If the total bill was for £300 then the journal to record the drawings would look like this:

Date	Details	Dr	Cr
2015		£	£
1st June	Drawings account	100	
	Telephone account		100
	Private use of telephone		

Notice how one third of the total phone bill has been transferred to drawings.

LEARNING POINT

Remember that journals only record the entries to be made in the main ledger. You must not draw up journals to record entries to subsidiary ledger accounts. So, if you have a Sales Ledger Control account, you must not show the entry to be made into the individual customer account, although you may record which account it is in the narrative.

Let us show the journal to write off a bad debt of one of our customers. Remember you would only write off a bad debt when you were given written authority to do this and you can only show the VAT if the debt is more than 6 months overdue.

Date	Details	Dr	Cr
2015		£	£
30th July	Bad debts account	150.00	
	VAT	30.00	
	Sales Ledger Control account		180.00
		180.00	180.00
	Outstanding amount on R Smith account written off as per memo from Finance Director.		

Another purpose of using a journal is to correct errors.

Suppose we recorded our electricity payment of £150 in the gas account. When the error comes to light we must never cross out entries and alter figures. That would be a recipe for fraud and in particular the auditor/tax man would not be too pleased.

Instead we should use a journal to record the correction of the error

Date	Details	Dr	Cr
2015		£	£
15th Aug	Electricity account	150	
	Gas account		150
	Correction of misposting electricity to the gas account		

You should note here that even if we recorded the VAT separately, we would not show it in this journal. The VAT would have been recorded correctly in the first place. It is not the VAT account which has the error, but the gas and electricity accounts.

You must be particularly careful where errors have been made by entering on the wrong side of the account. In such cases you must correct the error and then enter it correctly.

Let us suppose that we have issued a credit note for £200 to a customer and this has mistakenly been entered into our accounts as an invoice. Firstly we must establish what the incorrect entry was and reverse it. For simplicity we will ignore VAT for the moment.

The incorrect entry would have been:

Debit	Sales Ledger Control account
Credit	Sales

Date	Details	Dr	Cr
2015		£	£
15th Sept	Sales account	200	
	Sales Ledger Control account		200
	Sales Returns account	200	
	Sales Ledger Control account		200
		400	400
	Correction of error posting Credit Note 1234 to K Patel as Sales Invoice		

Of course, once you are accustomed to journals you may wish to show the Sales Ledger Control account only once with a credit entry of £400, but until you are used to it, it would be safer to use the method shown above.

EXAM ALERT!

Many marks have been lost in exams because the candidate has put the nature of the figure rather than what account it should be shown in. Journals show which **accounts** to debit and credit. Only the journal narrative explains what the journal has been created for.
The secret of success in your exams for journals which correct errors is to

a) Establish what the entries were in the original error

b) Decide what the correct entries should be

c) Decide what entries are needed to get from point a) to point b)

The Trial Balance (TB)

As we have seen every debit entry made in the double entry system must have a credit entry for the same amount. We have also seen how accounts are balanced and that this is done on a regular basis.

You are already probably aware that there will be a large number of accounts in an accounting system and we need some way of checking that our figures are correct from time to time. This checking is done by drawing up a **Trial Balance**. How often this is done will depend on the company, how many accounts there are and how many transactions in each account. Some larger companies will '*extract*' a Trial Balance weekly, but smaller companies may do this once a month.

CHAPTER 14

Journals and the Trial Balance

A Trial Balance is simply a list of **all** the accounts in an accounting system recorded as either a debit balance or a credit balance. This will mean, of course, balancing every account before the Trial Balance is extracted.

Of course, the balance b/d figure will show whether it is a debit or a credit balance, but you will be expected to know what it should be in most cases. We will look at this in a moment. First let us see what a Trial Balance will look like.

Trial Balance
30 September 2015

Name of account	Dr £	Cr £
Sales		15,000
Sales Returns	300	
Purchases	8,000	
Purchase Returns		150
Sales Ledger Control	2,000	
Purchases Ledger Control		1,000
Heat & Light	900	
Office Equipment	2,500	
Vehicle	8,000	
Stock (at 1st Jan 2011)	7,000	
Cash (till float)	200	
Bank	7,500	
VAT		1,250
Bank Loan		5,000
Capital		18,750
Drawings	4,750	
	41,150	**41,150**

We can see that each account is named and listed with its balance as a debit or a credit. Since we have only posted amounts as double entry into these main ledger accounts then the debits must match the credits.

We can also have a look at some accounts to see that they are roughly correct. Cash, for example, cannot be a credit entry. If it were it would mean that we had a negative amount of notes and coins on the premises – obviously this is not possible. A loan cannot be a debit. If it were it would mean that the bank would owe us.

CHAPTER 14
Journals and the Trial Balance

A few accounts can be either a debit or credit. The bank account will be a debit when we have sufficient funds there, but it will be a credit when we are overdrawn (have taken out more money than we have put in).

The VAT account can also be either. It will be a debit balance when we are due a refund and a credit balance when we owe amounts to HMRC.

These accounts are exceptions, and generally accounts will be always a debit or always a credit. Remembering which is which is one of the requirements of this Unit. Some of them you will already know. Sales are always credits while purchases are always debits. Some of them you may not be so sure of or have forgotten.

There are many ways people remember which is which, but one method is by using 'pearls'. You can use the letters of the word 'pearls' as an aid to remembering debits or credits.

Firstly you must split the letters into two halves – P E A and R L S

Start with the debits

P – Purchases. We have seen earlier in this book what a purchase is in accounting terms.

E – Expenses. Anything we pay out as a means of keeping the business running. This can include wages, phone bill, stationery, electricity. The accounting system sees it as goods and services we have brought into the business, just as if we can buy electricity in boxes from the shop. This is the 'receiving' part of the accounts (see p 50).

A – Assets. This will include fixed assets such as cars, property, machinery etc, and also includes stock and any cash we have on the premises. If we have money in the bank then this is also an asset. Our Sales Ledger Control is also an asset as it is money due to us.

Then we come to the credits

R – Revenue. This is the opposite of an expense. Revenue may be money we get from renting out spare office or warehouse space, or it may be the profit we make on selling our old car.

L – Liabilities. This is the opposite of an asset. Basically it is anything we owe. Bank loans and the Purchases ledger control come under this heading. If we are overdrawn at the bank then this will be a liability, just as if we owe money to HMRC for VAT or PAYE. We have seen on p 196 that the capital account is also a liability.

S – Sales. Anything we sell as part of our trade. Remember it doesn't have to be goods; it can be services.

One further point to remember is that a reduction in anything will be on the opposite side. Purchases are debits so Purchase Returns will be credits. Sales are credits so Sales Returns are debits.

IMPORTANT POINT

Learning what should be a debit and what should be a credit is essential to not only this unit but also all areas of accounting. Once you have mastered debits and credits then you are well on your way to success in this unit.

Checking the Trial Balance

We have seen that the Trial Balance must balance. But what if it doesn't? The first thing to do is to check that we haven't made a mistake when extracting the Trial Balance (TB). Points to look at are:

Has the total of the TB been calculated correctly
Has the balance on each account been correctly copied
Have **all** accounts been included
Find out by how much the totals differ. Halve the amount and look for an account with this amount. For example take the following accounts

	Dr	Cr
	£	£
Sales		1,000
Sales Returns		100
Purchases	500	
Bank	400	
	900	1,100

You can see that the difference is £200 (£1,100 - £900). If we halve this amount (£100) and look through the accounts we can see that the Sales Returns has this amount in it. We should also spot that this account is on the wrong side – it should be a debit balance. If we correct this and put the £100 into the debit column then the two sides will balance.

If the difference between the two totals is 9 or a multiple of 9 then the chances are that a figure has been reversed. 54 and 45 have a difference of 9. 102 and 120 have a difference of 18 (2 x 9). You can try out your own examples.

Suspense accounts

If the trial balance does not balance, then a **suspense account** will be raised. The suspense account is simply an account to hold errors. At first, the account will be debited or credited with the amount by which the TB is wrong. So if the TB has a debit balance of £100,000 and a credit balance of £99,000 then a suspense account will be raised with an opening credit balance of £1,000. Remember there will be no double entry for this as all we are doing at the moment is making the TB balance.

The suspense account is not one which lets us avoid finding out what the error is, but it will allow us time to find out what the error might be. You should never show a suspense account in your published figures.

> **LEARNING POINT**
>
> Correcting errors on the Trial Balance is not something which can be taught exactly. There is no formula or exact procedure. It is, however, an opportunity to show your knowledge of the double entry system. You must know how it should be done and then investigate to see how it has not been done properly. Raising a suspense account and then correcting the errors which caused the suspense account is a favourite topic in exams.

Let us take the example above of a suspense account with a credit balance of £1,000.

Dr		Suspense Account			Cr
Date	Details	£	Date	Details	£
			31/12/14	TB Difference	1000

Remember that this difference may be due to one error or it may be due to a number of errors. Therefore a detailed examination of the accounts must now be made.

Let us suppose that we find that the sales day book shows sales of £10,000, but the total column comes to £10,100. (We will assume there is no VAT for now to make things easier to see). Sales have been *undercast* (added up with a total too low) by £100. We need to add an extra £100 to the sales account.

Each time we find an error we use a journal to correct it. Remember that since we now have a suspense account part of the journal will be to this account.

Date	Details	Dr	Cr
2015		£	£
3rd Jan	Suspense account	100	
	Sales account		100
	Sales undercast now corrected		

Let us now suppose that we have found that the entry in the cash book for the payment of the electricity of £500 was **debited** instead of credited. We know that the electricity account was correctly debited. Here we must remove the error first and then enter it correctly.

Date	Details	Dr	Cr
2015		£	£
3rd Jan	Suspense account	500	
	Bank account		500
	Suspense account	500	
	Bank account		500
		1000	1000
	Payment of electricity debited to bank account in error		

You can see here that the £500 has first been taken out of the debit side and then put in the credit side.

LEARNING POINT

Be careful with errors of this type. Many students lose marks because they have only corrected the error. They forget to put through the correct entry afterwards.

Finally let us suppose we find an entry in the cash book for a cheque which has been raised for £100 but there is no explanation what it's for. Upon investigation we find that the owner of the business has taken the cheque out to buy his wife a Christmas present. Since this comes under money taken for personal use it must be classed as drawings. The journal entry should be:

Date	Details	Dr	Cr
2014		£	£
3rd Jan	Drawings account	100	
	Suspense account		100
	Cheque taken by owner for personal use		

If you remember, journals are books of prime entry, so these journals will need posting to the main ledger accounts. For now, though, we will look at just the suspense account entries.

Dr		Suspense Account			Cr
Date	Details	£	Date	Details	£
3/1/15	**Sales**	**100**	31/12/14	TB Difference	1000
3/1/15	**Bank**	**500**	**3/1/15**	**Drawings**	**100**
3/1/15	**Bank**	**500**			

The details columns show where the other side of the double entry took place.

We can now balance the suspense account

Dr		Suspense Account			Cr
Date	Details	£	Date	Details	£
3/1/15	Sales	100	31/12/14	TB Difference	1000
3/1/15	Bank	500	3/1/15	Drawings	100
3/1/15	Bank	500			
		1100			**1100**

We can see that there is now no balance on the suspense account and so our TB will balance properly without it.

Errors not shown by a Trial Balance

While the TB will show errors in the double entry, the TB cannot show that the figures are right. There will be errors that are not highlighted by the TB.

Error of omission. This is where a transaction has been completely omitted from the accounts. There will be neither a debit nor a credit entry

Reversal of entries. This is where the debit and credit entries have been entered on the wrong side of the accounts. For example if a cash sale is entered as a debit on the sales account and a credit in the bank account then the TB will not highlight the error, but nevertheless the entry is wrong

Error of commission. This is where the entry has been made in the wrong account. It could be that the electricity payment has been recorded in the stationery account

Error of principle. Similar to an error of commission except that the entry has been made in the wrong type of account. For example payment for fuel for the company van may have been entered in the vehicle cost account (a fixed asset account) but should be recorded in the vehicle running expense account (an expense account)

Error of original entry. This is where the correct accounts have been used with the correct sides of the account, but the wrong figure has been used. This may be due to a copying error or a bad figure on the invoice.

Compensating errors. This is where more than one error has been made but the errors add up to the same amount. For example:

	Dr	Cr
	£	£
Sales		1,000
Sales Returns		100
Purchases	500	
Purchase returns	200	
Bank	400	
	1,100	1,100

Here you can see that both the Sales Returns and the Purchases Returns are on the wrong side, but the TB still balances.

EXAM ALERT!

You will be expected to know which errors cause the TB not to balance and those that don't. You may be asked to prepare journals to correct errors and you will need to know whether to use the suspense account or not.

An error such as an entry in the cash book with no corresponding double entry will need a correction in the suspense account whereas the complete omission of an invoice will not as no double entry has been made at all.

If the original error causes the TB not to balance you will always use a suspense account. If the original error is such that the TB still balances you will **not** use a suspense account.

CHAPTER 14
Journals and the Trial Balance

International Terminology

Throughout this book the regular UK terminology has been used. However, international terminology is being used more and more. You will be expected to have a knowledge of both.

A comparison of the most common terms is given below.

UK		**International**
Fixed Assets	=	Non Current Assets
Stock	=	Inventory
Debtors	=	Receivables
Creditors	=	Payables
Profit and Loss Account	=	Statement of Profit or Loss
Balance Sheet	=	Statement of Financial Position

After the Trial Balance

Once the Trial Balance (TB) has been checked and we are happy that it is correct and that all errors and omissions have been found and corrected we will be ready to draw up the financial statements. This is covered in detail the AAT Level 3 Diploma, but for now we should know a summary of what happens next.

Some of the accounts in the TB will be used to draw up a **Profit & Loss** statement (a Statement of Profit or Loss). We have already seen that this comes in two parts; there is the **Trading Account** and the full **Profit & Loss Account**. The trading account shows what profit or loss a business has made in a given period by comparing the sales revenue with the cost of what it has sold. The full Profit & Loss account also compares the expense accounts such as electricity, vehicle running costs, stationery, rent etc.

Profit & Loss accounts cover a specific period of time. Some companies will draw up a P&L weekly or monthly, but usually a company will be required to draw up an annual P&L.

The P&L shows

INCOME minus EXPENSES equals PROFIT

CHAPTER 14

Journals and the Trial Balance

Those accounts not used in the P&L are used in the **Balance Sheet** (a Statement of Financial Position). A Balance Sheet shows what the business owns and what it owes at any one point in time.

Assets – this is what a business owns. It includes the fixed assets, the stock of goods for resale, the money owed by customers (debtors), money in the bank and money on the premises, and any money paid in advance (e.g. next month's rent)

Liabilities – this is what a business owes. It includes any loans, or any money owed to suppliers (creditors) or other bodies (e.g. HMRC for VAT or PAYE)

Capital – this is money which has been used to finance the business (also called *equity*).

The Balance Sheet shows

ASSETS minus LIABILITIES equals CAPITAL

This is known as the *accounting equation* and is the foundation of all double entry accounting.

You should know how financial transactions affect the accounting equation. Let us take a few examples.

If you open your business with £50,000 you will have

£50,000 ASSETS (money in the bank)

£50,000 CAPITAL

We have ASSETS (£50,000) *minus* LIABILITIES (£0) *equals* CAPITAL (£50,000)
If we then get a loan of £20,000 from the bank we have increased the assets by £20,000 as the money will go into the bank. We have increased liabilities by £20,000 because we owe the money back to the bank.

Our revised total will be

ASSETS (£70,000 made up of the money in the bank from the initial capital plus the money in the bank from the loan)

Minus LIABILITIES (£20,000 which is the amount of the loan)

Equals CAPITAL (£50,000).

Let us suppose that you next buy a delivery van for £20,000 on credit

The assets will increase by £20,000. The van itself is an asset. The liabilities will increase by £20,000 because we owe this money to the supplier (it was bought on credit you remember).

Our revised total will be

ASSETS (£90,000 made up of the money in the bank from the initial capital plus the money in the bank from the loan, plus the vehicle)

Minus LIABILITIES (£40,000 which is the amount of the bank loan, plus the amount you owe to the supplier of the van)

Equals CAPITAL (£50,000).

Be careful with transactions which increase and decrease assets at the same time. If you bought a new cash register for £500 for cash you would increase the assets by £500 - the cash register itself. You would decrease the assets (the money in the bank).

Our revised total will be

ASSETS (£90,000 made up of the money in the bank from the initial capital plus the money in the bank from the loan less the payment for the cash register, plus the vehicle plus the cash register)

Minus LIABILITIES (£40,000 which is the amount of the bank loan, plus the amount you owe to the supplier of the van)

Equals CAPITAL (£50,000).

LEARNING POINT

Remember that financial transactions **always** have two parts. You can never increase the total assets without increasing liabilities or capital or reducing other assets.

Chapter Summary

A journal is used as a book of prime entry to record less common transactions and to correct errors.

A Trial Balance (TB) is extracted at regular intervals to check the accuracy of the double entry in the main ledger accounts.

Some accounts will usually have debit balances while others will usually have credit balances. The bank account and the VAT account arc examples of accounts which may have balances on either side.

If the TB shows an error has been made then a suspense account will be drawn up to hold the amount by which the TB doesn't balance.

If a suspense account is drawn up, errors must be investigated immediately and corrected by means of a journal.

A suspense account will not normally be shown in the final financial statements.

Not all errors will be exposed by extracting a TB.

CHAPTER 14
Journals and the Trial Balance

Practice Questions

Chapter 14

14.1

The following transactions and transaction errors have occurred in the main ledger

a) The van servicing cost of £250.00 (excluding VAT) has been debited to the Vehicles : Cost account instead of the Vehicles Expense account.

b) The proprietor took some goods from the shop for his own use. The value of the goods was £100.00 (Ignore VAT).

c) A purchase for £600 + VAT has been debited to the Purchases Ledger Control and credited to the purchase account and the VAT account.

d) A cash sale for £165.00 has been entered in all the relevant accounts as £156.00 (Ignore VAT).

e) One of our customers has gone into liquidation. The whole of the Balance on the customer account is to be written off. The amount is £4,800 including VAT.

Show the journal entries to record these items

Today's date is 1st May 2015

Date	Details	Dr	Cr

Date	Details	Dr	Cr

Date	Details	Dr	Cr

Date	Details	Dr	Cr

Date	Details	Dr	Cr

14.2

The following is a list of balances as at 30 April 2015. The opening capital has been omitted. Prepare a Trial Balance and insert the missing capital account figure

Sales	£250,765
Sales Returns	£1,365
Debtors (SLC)	£36,527
Purchases	£107,650
Purchases Returns	£875
Creditors (PLC)	£26,298
Stock	£8,274
Office Equipment	£37,750

Company vehicles	£105,629
Bank Loan	£5,000
Bank	£1,279 (debit balance)
Wages expense	£2,350
Drawings	£10,000

Trial Balance
30 April 2015

Name of account	Dr £	Cr £
Sales		
Sales Returns		
Purchases		
Purchase Returns		
Sales Ledger Control		
Purchases Ledger Control		
Office Equipment		
Vehicles		
Stock		
Wages		
Bank		
Bank Loan		
Capital		
Drawings		

CHAPTER 14
Journals and the Trial Balance

14.3

Which of these errors will cause an imbalance on the Trial Balance?

a) The trade discount has been omitted from a sales invoice

b) A purchase invoice has been omitted from the accounts altogether

c) N Reed (a credit customer) has taken a settlement discount. This has been recorded in the main ledger correctly but not in the customer account in the subsidiary sales ledger

d) A cash purchase has been recorded in the cash book, but not in the purchases account or the VAT account

14.4

A Trial Balance has been extracted from the records, but fails to balance by £59. The amount is shown as a CR balance in a suspense account

Later the following errors are found:

a) The rent paid has been shown in the cash book but not the rent account. The amount is £250

b) The Purchases account has been overcast by £100

c) The cash book shows a payment of £45 for payment of the telephone, but this is shown as £54 in the telephone account. The cash book is correct.

d) A cash purchase for £200 has been shown correctly in the cash book, but it has been shown twice in the purchases account.

e) A payment of £250 from R Rivera (a credit customer) has been shown correctly in the cash book, the VAT account and the Sales Ledger Control, but has been omitted completely from the customer account in the Subsidiary Sales Ledger.

Make the journal entries to correct these errors (the date is 31st May 2015)

Show the suspense account after the errors have been corrected

CHAPTER 14
Journals and the Trial Balance

Date	Details	Dr	Cr
		£	£

Date	Details	Dr	Cr
		£	£

Date	Details	Dr	Cr
		£	£

Date	Details	Dr	Cr
		£	£

Date	Details	Dr	Cr

Dr		Suspense Account			Cr
Date	Details	£	Date	Details	£
				TB Difference	59

(This page is left blank for your notes)

Summary

This book has shown that businesses need to record financial transactions and present them in a basically standard form.

While the recording and documenting has variations from business to business, there will be a basic process which follows a number of stages:

PRIME DOCUMENTS

These are the source documents of the transactions. They will include:

- Invoices
- Credit Notes
- Purchase Orders
- Cheques
- Till rolls

↓

BOOKS OF PRIME ENTRY

These gather the information given by the prime documents. They include:

- Day Books
- Cash Books
- Journals

↓

DOUBLE ENTRY ACCOUNTS

This is where the transactions (or summary of the transactions) are recorded in the main accounting ledgers. These include:

Main Ledger
Cash Books

(You must remember that some accounts in the main ledger are a summary of subsidiary ledgers. While these subsidiary ledgers are not part of the double entry, they must be updated so that the summary account (or control account) will match the total of the subsidiary accounts of which they are a summary).

TRIAL BALANCE

This is where the double entry bookkeeping is checked for arithmetical errors. It is a summary of **all** the accounts in the double entry system.

FINANCIAL STATEMENTS

This includes:

Profit & Loss Account – where the profit or loss for any given accounting period is calculated.

Balance Sheet – which states the assets, liabilities and capital of a business at a particular point in time.

Answers to Practice Questions

Chapter 1

1.1
a) Sole Trader
b) Limited Company
c) Partnership
d) Public Limited Company (plc)

1.2
a) a) and c)
b) b) and c)

1.3
a) b
b) c
c) a

Chapter 2

2.1
a) Invoice
b) Statement
c) Quote
d) Purchase Order
e) Delivery Note
f) Returns Note
g) Credit Note

2.2
a) Errors and Omissions Excepted. It means that if a genuine error has been made, then the person cannot be held to it.

b) The price of the goods does not include delivery

c) Cash on Delivery. Payment must be made when the goods are delivered

2.3

	Total	Discount	Net total	VAT	Gross total
	£	£	£	£	£
a)	1750.00	525.00	1225.00	245.00	1470.00
b)	525.00	0.00	525.00	105.00	630.00
c)	35000.00	10500.00	24500.00	4900.00	29400.00

2.4

	Total	Discount	Net total	VAT	Gross total
	£	£	£	£	£
a)	1750.00	525.00	1225.00	237.65	1462.65
b)	525.00	0.00	525.00	101.85	626.85
c)	35000.00	10500.00	24500.00	4753.00	29253.00

2.5 a) £1425.90
b) £611.10
c) £28518.00

2.6 a) £350.00
b) £67.90
c) £417.90

2.7

STATEMENT OF ACCOUNT
T&T Ltd

154 Margaret St, Immingham, IM17 9RQ

To

G Stephens
65 Dudley Road
Birmingham
B5 4BL

Account GS01

Date 31st Nov 2014

Date	Details	Debit £	Credit £	Balance £
1/11/14	Balance b/f	325.50		325.50
6/11/14	Inv 23469	650.00		975.50
7/11/14	Payment		317.00	658.50
7/11/14	Discount		8.50	650.00
21/11/14	Inv 23576	700.00		1350.00
22/11/14	CN 57		50.00	1300.00

TOTAL AMOUNT OUTSTANDING **1300.00**

Chapter 3

3.1 a) £35.00
b) £0.07
c) £0.29
d) £3032.03
e) £55.95

3.2 Agreement
Consideration
Intention to create legal relations

3.3 No. The price in the paper is just an invitation to treat. The offer is made at the till.

3.4 No. You have made a counter offer by altering the terms.

3.5 No. There was no intention to create legal relations. The payment of £10 was incidental and moreover it was paid after the event.

3.6 No. The fact that it was in the sale makes no difference to the purchaser's rights unless the fault was made known at the time of purchase.

3.7 No. If it was advertised as adjustable then it must be adjustable. You could report them to the Trading Standards Institute.

3.8 No. A receipt is not necessary and signs put up in shops cannot override consumer rights. The shopkeeper would expect some proof that the goods were bought from the shop, but in this case there is ample evidence.

3.9 Performance
Agreement
Frustration
Breach of contract

3.10 Yes. The Sale of Goods Act does not cover traders in the same way as consumers. Had the customer bought the goods directly from the supplier then the supplier would have had to repair or replace the goods if at all possible.

Chapter 4

4.1

SALES DAY BOOK **SDB 101**

Date	Invoice	Customer	Folio	Total		Sales		VAT	
2015				£	p	£	p	£	p
5th Jan	23579	M Harvey	SL 23	60	00	50	00	10	00
5th Jan	23580	N Pearson	SL 52	91	20	76	00	15	20
6th Jan	23581	P Murray	SL 45	134	40	112	00	22	40
7th Jan	23582	M Harvey	SL 23	90	00	75	00	15	00
7th Jan	23583	R Graham	SL 15	118	80	99	00	19	80
8th Jan	23584	P Murray	SL 45	54	00	45	00	9	00
9th Jan	23585	S Walsh	SL 79	96	00	80	00	16	00
9th Jan	23586	M Harvey	SL 23	66	00	55	00	11	00
9th Jan		**TOTAL FOR THE WEEK**		**710**	**40**	**592**	**00**	**118**	**40**

4.2, 4.4 & 4.5

SALES LEDGER

Dr	**R Graham Account (SL 15)**				Cr
Date	Details	£	Date	Details	£
7th Jan	Inv 23583	118.80	9th Jan	Balance c/d	118.80
		118.80			118.80
10th Jan	Balance b/d	118.80			

Dr		M Harvey Account (SL 23)			Cr
Date	Details	£	Date	Details	£
5th Jan	Inv 23579	60.00	6th Jan	CN 239	24.00
7th Jan	Inv 23582	90.00	9th Jan	Balance c/d	192.00
9th Jan	Inv 23586	66.00			
		216.00			216.00
10th Jan	Balance b/d	192.00			

Dr		P Murray Account (SL 45)			Cr
Date	Details	£	Date	Details	£
6th Jan	Inv 23581	134.40	8th Jan	CN 240	20.40
8th Jan	Inv 23584	54.00	9th Jan	Balance c/d	168.00
		188.40			188.40
10th Jan	Balance b/d	168.00			

Dr		N Pearson Account (SL 52)			Cr
Date	Details	£	Date	Details	£
5th Jan	Inv 23580	91.20	9th Jan	Balance c/d	91.20
		91.20			91.20
10th Jan	Balance b/d	91.20			

Dr		S Walsh Account (SL 79)			Cr
Date	Details	£	Date	Details	£
9th Jan	Inv 23585	96.00	9th Jan	Balance c/d	96.00
		96.00			96.00
10th Jan	Balance b/d	96.00			

MAIN LEDGER

Dr		Sales Account (4000)			Cr
Date	Details	£	Date	Details	£
9th Jan	Balance c/d	592.00	9th Jan	SDB 101	592.00
		592.00			592.00
			10th Jan	Balance b/d	592.00

Dr	Sales Returns Account (4050)				Cr
Date	Details	£	Date	Details	£
9th Jan	SRDB 12	37.00	9th Jan	Balance c/d	37.00
		37.00			37.00
10th Jan	Balance b/d	37.00			

Dr	VAT Account (2200)				Cr
Date	Details	£	Date	Details	£
9th Jan	SRDB 12	7.40	9th Jan	SDB 101	118.40
9th Jan	Balance c/d	111.00			
		118.40			118.40
			10th Jan	Balance b/d	111.00

Dr	Sales Ledger Control Account (1100)				Cr
Date	Details	£	Date	Details	£
9th Jan	SDB 101	710.40	9th Jan	SRDB 12	44.40
			9th Jan	Balance c/d	666.00
		710.40			710.40
10th Jan	Balance b/d	666.00			

4.3

SALES RETURNS DAY BOOK **SRDB 12**

Date	Cr Note	Customer	Folio	Total		Sales		VAT	
				£	p	£	p	£	p
2015									
6th Jan	CN239	M Harvey	SL 23	24	00	20	00	4	00
8th Jan	CN240	P Murray	SL 45	20	40	17	00	3	40
9th Jan		**TOTAL FOR THE WEEK**		**44**	**40**	**37**	**00**	**7**	**40**

Reconciliation of Sales Ledger Control Account
9th January 2015

	£	£
R Graham	118.80	
M Harvey	192.00	
P Murray	168.00	
N Pearson	91.20	
S Walsh	96.00	
TOTAL	**666.00**	
TOTAL PER SALES LEDGER CONTROL		**666.00**
Discrepancy (if any)	nil	

Chapter 5

5.1

CASHBOOK - RECEIPTS — CBR35

Date	Detail	Folio	Discount Allowed		Bank		Cash Sale		VAT		Sales Ledger		Other Income	
2015			£	p	£	p	£	p	£	p	£	p	£	p
2nd Feb	Bal b/d				650	00								
2nd Feb	R Burch	SL17			616	87					616	87		
2nd Feb	Cash Sale	ML 4000			960	00	800	00	160	00				
3rd Feb	J Kovacs	SL29	50	00	293	75					293	75		
4th Feb	Rent	ML 4904			120	00							120	00
4th Feb	Cash Sale	ML 4000			624	00	520	00	104	00				
5th Feb	Cash Sale	ML 4000			138	00	115	00	23	00				
5th Feb	F Sinclair	SL40	50	00	881	25					881	25		
6th Feb	Cash Sale	ML 4000			510	00	425	00	85	00				
			100	**00**	**4793**	**87**	**1860**	**00**	**372**	**00**	**1791**	**87**	**120**	**00**

5.2

SALES LEDGER

Dr		R Burch Account (SL 17)			Cr
Date	Details	£	Date	Details	£
			02/02/15	CRB 35	616.87

Dr		J Kovacs Account (SL 29)			Cr
Date	Details	£	Date	Details	£
			03/02/15	CRB 35	293.75
			03/02/15	Disc Allowed	50.00

Dr		F Sinclair Account (SL 40)			Cr
Date	Details	£	Date	Details	£
			05/02/15	CRB 35	881.25
			05/02/15	Disc Allowed	50.00

MAIN LEDGER

Dr		Sales Account (4000)			Cr
Date	Details	£	Date	Details	£
			06/02/15	CBR35	1860.00

Dr		Rent Received Account (4904)			Cr
Date	Details	£	Date	Details	£
			06/02/15	CBR35	120.00

Dr		VAT Account (2200)			Cr
Date	Details	£	Date	Details	£
			06/02/15	CBR35	372.00

Dr		Sales Ledger Control Account (1100)			Cr
Date	Details	£	Date	Details	£
			06/02/15	CBR35	1791.87
			06/02/15	Disc Allowed	100.00

Dr		Discounts Allowed Account (4009)			Cr
Date	Details	£	Date	Details	£
06/02/15	CBR35	100.00			

5.3

a) i) No date
ii) No signature
iii) Figures and words don't match

b) Chigley Bank plc

c) It means that the cheque can only be paid into the payee's bank account

5.4

The debit card is linked directly to the customer's bank account. A credit card payment will be notified to the customer's bank and a statement will be sent to the customer monthly.

5.5

a) Bankers Automated Clearing Service
b) Electronic Funds Transfer at Point Of Sale
c) Clearing House Automated Payment System
d) Faster Payments Service

Chapter 6

6.1

Denomination	Quantity	Total £
£50	0	0
£20	6	120.00
£10	9	90.00
£5	8	40.00
£1	27	27.00
50p	12	6.00
20p	15	3.00
10p	36	3.60
5p	8	0.40
2p	6	0.12
1p	15	0.15
		290.27

(Note: you are not paying in the notes and coins you need for the next day's float)

Date *6th February 2015*

Please detail cheques and slips on the back

Cashier's stamp

Bank Giro Credit

IMMINGHAM BANK plc
14 Springfield Road, Brigg, DN20 3GF
Account
Dawson Supplies
Paid in by *Your signature*

NUMBER OF CHEQUES/ SLIPS *2*

	£	p
£50		
£20	*120*	*00*
£10	*70*	*00*
£5	*30*	*00*
£1	*17*	*00*
50p	*1*	*00*
Silver	*2*	*20*
Bronze	*0*	*07*
TOTAL CASH	*240*	*27*
Cheque/slips	*670*	*00*
£	*910*	*27*

Sort Code	Account Number
01-26-73	54379654

Paying in slip (front)

Details of cheques/slips	Amount £	p
G Bell	*170*	*00*
N Hussain	*500*	*00*
Total cheques/slips carried over	*670*	*00*

Paying in slip (back)

6.2

An overdraft is usually to cover day-to-day expenses and will vary regularly according to the needs of the customer. A loan is different in that it is usually used to cover purchases of specific items. The money is paid back in regular instalments.

6.3

A current account

6.4

1. Cheques that the company has written may not have been presented at the bank yet

2. Cheques may not have completed the clearing system yet

3. Bank charges may have been made by the bank, but are not yet recorded in the cash book

4. Interest paid by the bank will not yet be shown in the cash book

5. Cash and cheques that have been paid into the bank may have been too late for inclusion in the statement.

Chapter 7

7.1

ii), iv), i), iii), v)

7.2 & 7.3

PURCHASES DAY BOOK **PDB 57**

Date	Invoice	Supplier	Folio	Total		Purchases		Other expenses		VAT	
2015				£	p	£	p	£	p	£	p
6th Feb	23571	L Butler	PL 15	600	00	500	00			100	00
6th Feb	7596	B Knight	PL 25	540	00	450	00			90	00
6th Feb	3964	M Barnes	PL 7	240	00	200	00			40	00
6th Feb	93678	H Lloyd	PL 31	60	00			50	00	10	00
6th Feb	57465	D Mills	PL 46	330	00	275	00			55	00
		TOTAL		**1770**	**00**	**1425**	**00**	**50**	**00**	**295**	**00**

PURCHASES RETURNS DAY BOOK **PRDB 03**

Date	Cr Note	Supplier	Folio	Total		Purchases returns		Other returns		VAT	
2015				£	p	£	p	£	p	£	p
9th Feb	CN 537	M Barnes	PL 7	48	00	40	00			8	00
9th Feb	RT 335	B Knight	PL 25	36	00	30	00			6	00
		TOTAL		**84**	**00**	**70**	**00**			**14**	**00**

PURCHASES LEDGER

Dr		M Barnes Account (PL 7)			Cr
Date	Details	£	Date	Details	£
09/02/15	PRDB 03	48.00	06/02/15	PDB 57	240.00
09/02/15	Balance c/d	192.00			
		240.00			240.00
			10/02/15	Balance b/d	192.00

Dr		L Butler Account (PL 15)			Cr
Date	Details	£	Date	Details	£
09/02/15	Balance c/d	600.00	06/02/15	PDB 57	600.00
		600.00			600.00
			10/02/15	Balance b/d	600.00

Dr		B Knight Account (PL 25)			Cr
Date	Details	£	Date	Details	£
09/02/15	PRDB 03	36.00	06/02/15	PDB 57	540.00
09/02/15	Balance c/d	504.00			
		540.00			540.00
			10/02/15	Balance b/d	504.00

Dr		H Lloyd Account (PL 31)			Cr
Date	Details	£	Date	Details	£
09/02/15	Balance c/d	60.00	06/02/15	PDB 57	60.00
		60.00			60.00
			10/02/15	Balance b/d	60.00

Dr		D Mills Account (PL 46)			Cr
Date	Details	£	Date	Details	£
09/02/15	Balance c/d	330.00	06/02/15	PDB 57	330.00
		330.00			330.00
			10/02/15	Balance b/d	330.00

MAIN LEDGER

Dr			Purchases		Cr
Date	Details	£	Date	Details	£
06/02/15	PDB 57	1425.00	09/02/15	Balance c/d	1425.00
		1425.00			1425.00
10/02/15	Balance b/d	1425.00			

Dr			Purchases Returns		Cr
Date	Details	£	Date	Details	£
09/02/15	Balance c/d	70.00	09/02/15	PRDB 03	70.00
		70.00			70.00
			10/02/15	Balance b/d	70.00

Dr			Other expenses		Cr
Date	Details	£	Date	Details	£
06/02/15	PDB 57	50.00	09/02/15	Balance c/d	50.00
		50.00			50.00
10/02/15	Balance b/d	50.00			

Dr			VAT Account		Cr
Date	Details	£	Date	Details	£
06/02/15	PDB 57	295.00	09/02/15	PRDB 03	14.00
			09/02/15	Balance c/d	281.00
		295.00			295.00
10/02/15	Balance b/d	281.00			

Dr			Purchases Ledger Control Account		Cr
Date	Details	£	Date	Details	£
09/02/15	PRDB 03	84.00	06/02/15	PDB 57	1770.00
09/02/15	Balance c/d	1686.00			
		1770.00			1770.00
			10/02/15	Balance b/d	1686.00

Chapter 8

8.1

Dawson Supplies

45 Scartho Street, Immingham, IM15 2BH

Remittance advice

Supplier: Barton Supplies

Date	Transaction ref	Amount (£)
09/02/15	Inv 5298	176.25
16/02/15	Inv 5420	528.75
23/02/15	Inv 5550	352.50
25/02/15	CN 259	(58.75)
09/03/15	Discount	(24.96)

CHEQUE TOTAL **973.79**

IMMINGHAM BANK plc

14 Springfield Road, Brigg, DN20 3GF

30 - 25 - 81

Date *9th March 2015*

Pay *Barton Supplies*

Nine hundred and seventy three

Pounds and 79 pence

A/C Payee

£ *973.79*

S Craggs

Cheque number 001481

Sort Code 30-25-81

Account number 12560798

8.2

1. Bank Giro credit
2. Company Credit Card
3. CHAPS
4. BACS
5. Banker's draft

(Note: other payments are possible, but these are the most appropriate)

8.3

CASHBOOK - PAYMENTS CBP83

Date	Detail	Discount Received		Bank		Cash Purchases		VAT		Purchases Ledger		Other Expenses	
		£	p	£	p	£	p	£	p	£	p	£	p
02/03/15	J Austin (Chq 567259)			293	75					293	75		
02/03/15	Travel (Chq 567260)			65	00							65	00
03/03/15	Rent (Chq 567261)			250	00							250	00
04/03/15	K Slater (Chq 567262)	12	50	572	81					572	81		
04/03/15	Cash purchase (Chq 567263)			96	00	80	00	16	00				
05/03/15	Stationery (Chq 567264)			66	00			11	00			55	00
05/03/15	L Doyle (Chq 267265)	11	87	556	04					556	04		
06/03/15	Wages (Chq 267266)			250	00							250	00
		24	**37**	**2149**	**60**	**80**	**00**	**27**	**00**	**1422**	**60**	**620**	**00**

PURCHASES LEDGER

Dr		J Austin Account			Cr
Date	Details	£	Date	Details	£
02/03/15	CBP 83	293.75			

Dr		K Slater Account			Cr
Date	Details	£	Date	Details	£
04/03/15	CBP 83	572.81			
04/03/15	Disc received	12.50			

Dr		L Doyle Account			Cr
Date	Details	£	Date	Details	£
05/03/15	CBP 83	556.04			
05/03/15	Disc received	11.87			

MAIN LEDGER

Dr		Purchases			Cr
Date	Details	£	Date	Details	£
06/03/15	CBP 83	80.00			

Dr		Other expenses			Cr
Date	Details	£	Date	Details	£
06/03/15	CBP 83	620.00			

Dr		VAT Account			Cr
Date	Details	£	Date	Details	£
06/03/15	CBP 83	27.00			

Dr		Purchases Ledger Control Account			Cr
Date	Details	£	Date	Details	£
06/03/15	CBP 83	1422.60			
06/03/15	Disc received	24.37			

Dr		Discounts Received Account			Cr
Date	Details	£	Date	Details	£
			06/03/15	CBP 83	24.37

8.4

PURCHASES DAY BOOK **PDB 87**

Date	Invoice	Customer	Total		Purchases		Other expenses		VAT	
2015			£	p	£	p	£	p	£	P
1st April	2359	H Nelson	240	00	200	00			40	00
2nd April	7963	F Drake	420	00	350	00			70	00
3rd April	432	J Cook	120	00	100	00			20	00
4th April	2368	H Nelson	300	00	250	00			50	00
		TOTAL	**1080**	**00**	**900**	**00**			**180**	**00**

PURCHASES RETURNS DAY BOOK **PRDB 05**

Date	Cr Note	Customer	Total		Purchases returns		Other returns		VAT	
			£	p	£	p	£	p	£	p
2015										
2nd April	CN 59	J Cook	60	00	50	00			10	00
		TOTAL	**60**	**00**	**50**	**00**			**10**	**00**

MAIN LEDGER

Dr		Purchases			Cr
Date	Details	£	Date	Details	£
01/04/15	Balance b/d	5600.00	04/04/15	Balance c/d	6500.00
04/04/15	PDB 87	900.00			
		6500.00			6500.00
05/04/15	Balance b/d	6500.00			

Dr		Purchases Returns			Cr
Date	Details	£	Date	Details	£
04/04/15	Balance c/d	200.00	01/04/15	Balance b/d	150.00
			04/04/15	PRDB 05	50.00
		200.00			200.00
			05/04/15	Balance b/d	200.00

Dr		VAT Account			Cr
Date	Details	£	Date	Details	£
01/04/15	Balance b/d	460.00	04/04/15	PRDB 05	10.00
04/04/15	PDB 87	180.00	04/04/15	Balance c/d	630.00
		640.00			640.00
05/04/15	Balance b/d	630.00			

Dr		Purchases Ledger Control Account			Cr
Date	Details	£	Date	Details	£
04/04/15	PRDB	60.00	01/04/15	Balance b/d	1095.00
04/04/15	Contra SLC	175.00	04/04/15	PDB 87	1080.00
04/04/15	Balance c/d	1940.00			
		2175.00			2175.00
			05/04/15	Balance b/d	1940.00

PURCHASES LEDGER

Dr		H Nelson Account			Cr
Date	Details	£	Date	Details	£
04/04/15	Balance c/d	930.00	01/04/15	Balance b/d	390.00
			01/04/15	PDB 87	240.00
			04/04/15	PDB 87	300.00
		930.00			930.00
			05/04/15	Balance b/d	930.00

Dr		J Cook Account			Cr
Date	Details	£	Date	Details	£
02/04/15	PRDB 05	60.00	01/04/15	Balance b/d	425.00
04/04/15	Contra SL	175.00	03/04/15	PDB 87	120.00
04/04/15	Balance c/d	310.00			
		545.00			545.00
			05/04/15	Balance b/d	310.00

Dr		F Drake Account			Cr
Date	Details	£	Date	Details	£
04/04/15	Balance c/d	700.00	01/04/15	Balance b/d	280.00
			02/04/15	PDB 87	420.00
		700.00			700.00
			05/04/15	Balance b/d	700.00

Reconciliation of Purchases Ledger Control Account
4th April 2015

	£	£
H Nelson	930.00	
J Cook	310.00	
F Drake	700.00	
TOTAL	**1940.00**	
TOTAL PER PURCHASES LEDGER CONTROL		**1940.00**
Discrepancy (if any)	nil	

Chapter 9

9.1

Petty Cash Voucher No 0465

Date prepared 09/04/15

Expenditure	Amount (£)
Postage Stamps	3.60
VAT	0.00
TOTAL	£ 3.60

Paid to A Begum

Authorised A Student

Petty Cash Voucher No 0466

Date prepared 09/04/15

Expenditure	Amount (£)
Taxi fare	5.00
VAT	1.00
TOTAL	£ 6.00

Paid to C Murph

Authorised A Student

Petty Cash Voucher **No 0467**

Date prepared 09/04/15

Expenditure	Amount (£)
Tea & Coffee	8.75
VAT	0.00
TOTAL	£ 8.75

Paid to K Ali

Authorised A Student

T Simpson's new Laser Toner cartridge receipt is above the authorisation limit. An expenses claim form will have to be filled in

S Marshall's taxi to work is not a business expense. He must pay this himself.

9.2

Petty Cash Book															PCB17
Receipts		Date	Detail	Voucher Number	Total		Analysis Columns								
							VAT		Travel		Stationery		Postage		
£	p	2015			£	p	£	p	£	p	£	p	£	p	
50	00	13th Apr	Balance b/d												
		13th Apr	Taxi	157	7	00	1	16	5	84					
		13th Apr	Photocopy Paper	158	20	40	3	40			17	00			
		14th April	Postage	159	0	75							0	75	
		15th April	Pens	160	2	40	0	40			2	00			
		16th April	Envelopes	161	5	40	0	90			4	50*			
		17th April	Train fare	162	10	50			10	50					
46	45	17th April	Cash received												
		17th April	Balance c/d		50	00									
96	**45**				**96**	**45**	5	86	16	34	23	50	0	75	
50	00	18th April	Balance b/d												

* Students may well have shown the envelopes in the 'postage' columns. This is equally correct. Where to show items is whatever is best for the business – there are no hard and fast rules.

Chapter 10

10.1

a) £19,238

b) £5,478

c) £1,600

d)

Dr	Wages Expense Account				Cr
Date	Details	£	Date	Details	£
30/04/15	Wages Control	16,800			
30/04/15	Employer NICs	1638			
30/04/15	Emp'er Pension	800			

Dr	Wages Control Account				Cr
Date	Details	£	Date	Details	£
30/04/15	Bank	12160	30/04/15	Wages Exp	16,800
30/04/15	PAYE	2816	30/04/15	Employer NICs	1638
30/04/15	NICs Emp'ee	1024	30/04/15	Emp'er Pension	800
30/04/15	NICs Emp'er	1638			
30/04/15	Pension Emp'ee	800			
30/04/15	Pension Emp'er	800			

Dr	Bank Account				Cr
Date	Details	£	Date	Details	£
			30/04/15	Net Wages	12160

Dr	HMRC Account				Cr
Date	Details	£	Date	Details	£
			30/04/15	PAYE	2816
			30/04/15	NICs Emp'ee	1024
			30/04/15	NICs Emp'er	1638

Dr	Pension Fund Account				Cr
Date	Details	£	Date	Details	£
			30/04/15	Pension Emp'ee	800
			30/04/15	Pension Emp'er	800

10.2

a) Amounts to be paid to HMRC

b) Amounts to be paid to the pension fund

c) 19th May for HMRC and 18th May for pension.

(Students will not be expected to know when the pension must be paid at this level. The question is given here as supplementary knowledge and understanding)

Chapter 11

11.1

a)

'Cc' stands for 'carbon copy' and it tells you that a copy of the memo has gone to this person.

'Bcc' stands for 'blind carbon copy' whereby the recipient is not made aware that a copy has been sent to anyone else.

b)

Fax

11.2

DAWSON SUPPLIES

45 Scartho Street,
Immingham,
IM15 2BH

T&T
154 Margaret Street,
Immingham,
IM17 9RQ

1st May 2015

Dear Mr Singh:

Overdue order

We understand that there has been a delay in processing your order for 20 rolls of fabric. We apologise for the delay but have discovered that we only received the Purchase Order 2 days ago.

We will endeavour to process this order as soon as possible and it should be with you no later than the middle of next week. Please be assured that your order will be treated as a priority.

I am enclosing a copy of the purchase order

Yours sincerely

Mr A Student

Encl. Copy purchase order

(Students are not expected to have exactly the same words, but essential features are the layout, naming the recipient, politeness, concise, the salutation (Yours sincerely) and stating the enclosures if there are any. There should be no blame placed on T&T)

Chapter 12

12.1

CASH BOOK

RECEIPTS | PAYMENTS

Date	Detail	Bank		Date	Detail	Bank	
2015		£				£	
6th Apr	Capital	5000	00	6th Apr	Office furniture	2400	00
13th Apr	Advertising income	60	00	6th Apr	Office equipment	960	00
13th Apr	Bank Loan	4000	00	13th Apr	Rent	150	00
20th Apr	Advertising income	60	00	17th Apr	Drawings	100	00
27th Apr	Advertising income	60	00	24th Apr	Drawings	150	00
				27th Apr	Loan repayment	100	00

Dr		Capital Account			Cr
Date	Details	£	Date	Details	£
			06/04/15	Bank	5000.00

Dr		VAT Account			Cr
Date	Details	£	Date	Details	£
06/04/15	Cash book	400.00	13/04/15	Cash book	10.00
06/04/15	Cash book	160.00	20/04/15	Cash book	10.00
			27/04/15	Cash book	10.00

Dr		Office Furniture Account			Cr
Date	Details	£	Date	Details	£
06/04/15	Cash book	2000.00			

Dr		Office Equipment Account			Cr
Date	Details	£	Date	Details	£
06/04/15	Cash book	800.00			

Dr		Rent Paid Account			Cr
Date	Details	£	Date	Details	£
13/04/15	Cash book	150.00			

Dr		Advertising Receivable Account			Cr
Date	Details	£	Date	Details	£
			13/04/15	Cash book	50.00
			20/04/15	Cash book	50.00
			27/04/15	Cash book	50.00

Dr		Bank Loan Account			Cr
Date	Details	£	Date	Details	£
27/04/15	Cash book	67.00	13/04/15	Cash book	4000.00

Dr		Drawings Account			Cr
Date	Details	£	Date	Details	£
17/04/15	Cash book	100.00			
24/04/15	Cash book	150.00			

Dr		Interest Payable Account			Cr
Date	Details	£	Date	Details	£
27/04/15	Cash book	33.00			

12.2

Dr		**VAT Account**			Cr
Date	Details	£	Date	Details	£
06/04/15	Cash book	400.00	13/04/15	Cash book	10.00
06/04/15	Cash book	160.00	20/04/15	Cash book	10.00
			27/04/15	Cash book	10.00
			30/04/15	Balance c/d	530.00
		560.00			560.00
01/05/15	Balance b/d	530.00			

£530.00 is due **from** HMRC.

12.3

Debit	Bad Debts Written off	£2,000
Debit	VAT	£400
Credit	Sales Ledger Control	£2,400

(The individual customer account for G Lopez will also need to be credited with £2,400)

12.4

a), b) and c) are capital. d) is revenue

Chapter 13

13.1

CASH BOOK

RECEIPTS | PAYMENTS

Date	Detail	Bank		Date	Detail	Bank	
2015		£				£	
1st May	Balance b/d	3502	72	3rd May	G Evans Chq 379652	741	00
1st May	Cash deposit	1352	00	3rd May	H Edwards Chq 379653	421	65
27th May	Cash deposit	1279	56	3rd May	J Collins Chq 379654	257	50
29th May	Cash deposit	236	57	8th May	K Stewart Chq 379655	175	25
18th May	*P Green*	*2475*	*00*	8th May	L Sanchez Chq 379656	1251	27
				18th May	M Morris Chq 379657	250	00
				26th May	P Rogers Chq 379658	729	57
				29th May	*Bank Charges*	*83*	*65*
				31st May	*Balance c/d*	*4935*	*96*
		8845	*85*			*8845*	*85*
1st June	*Balance c/d*	*4935*	*96*				

Bank Reconciliation Statement
31 May 2015

	£	£
Balance as per bank statement		**5850.61**
Less: unpresented cheques		
379653	421.65	
379658	729.57	
		1151.22
		4699.39
Add: outstanding lodgements		
	236.57	
		236.57
Balance as per cash book		4935.96

Chapter 14

14.1

Date	Details	Dr	Cr

2015		£	£
1st May	Vehicles Expense	250.00	
	Vehicles: Cost		250.00
	Correction of misposting		
Date	Details	Dr	Cr
2015		£	£
1st May	Drawings	100.00	
	Purchases *		100.00
	Stock taken for own use		
Date	Details	Dr	Cr
2015		£	£
1st May	Purchases	600.00	
	VAT	120.00	
	Purchases Ledger Control		720.00
	Purchases	600.00	
	VAT	120.00	
	Purchases Ledger Control		720.00
	Correction of reversal of entries		
Date	Details	Dr	Cr
2015		£	£
1st May	Sales	156.00	
	Cash Book (or Bank, or cash)		156.00
	Cash Book (or Bank, or cash)**	165.00	
	Sales		165.00
	Correction of transposition of figures		
Date	Details	Dr	Cr
2015		£	£
1st May	Bad debts	4,000.00	
	VAT	800.00	
	Sales Ledger Control		4,800.00
	Customer one into liquidation		

* It is incorrect to adjust 'stock' account. Stock accounts will be physically counted at the beginning and end of each period. As the goods have been taken away they are no longer 'purchases'. (See p197).

** Alternatively debit cash book with £9 and credit the sales with £9.

14.2

Trial Balance
30 April 2015

Name of account	Dr £	Cr £
Sales		250,765
Sales Returns	1,365	
Purchases	107,650	
Purchase Returns		875
Sales Ledger Control	36,527	
Purchases Ledger Control		26,298
Office Equipment	37,750	
Vehicles	105,629	
Stock	8,274	
Wages	2,350	
Bank	1,279	
Bank Loan		5,000
Capital		**27,886**
Drawings	10,000	
	310,824	**310,824**

14.3

Only d) will cause an imbalance

14.4

Date	Details	Dr	Cr
2015		£	£
31st	Rent	250.00	
May	Suspense		250.00
	Omission of posting to rent account		

Date	Details	Dr	Cr
2015		£	£
31st	Suspense	100.00	
May	Purchases		100.00
	Correction of overcast purchases account		

Date	Details	Dr	Cr
2015		£	£
31st	Suspense	9.00	
May	Telephone		9.00
	Correction of transposition error		

Date	Details	Dr	Cr
2015		£	£
31st	Suspense	200.00	
May	Purchases		200.00
	Correction of showing purchase twice in purchase account		

Date	Details	Dr	Cr

(Note: error (e) does not need a journal since it will not affect the main ledger at all)

Dr		**Suspense Account**			Cr
Date	Details	£	Date	Details	£
31/05/15	Purchases	100	31/05/15	TB Difference	59
31/05/15	Telephone	9	31/05/15	Rent	250
31/05/15	Purchases	200			
		309			309

Answers to Practice Questions

INDEX

accountant	1, 4, 6	bank account	49, 101-102, 105
accounting equation	236-237	bank giro credit	133
accounting technician	2, 5, 6, 50, 183	bank statement	49, 105-107, 211-219
advice note	13	banker's draft	93
agent	102	batch control	124
BACS	89-90, 174	book of prime entry	1, 48, 197, 223
bad debt	201, 225-226	bookkeeper	1,2,4
bailee	102	building society	101
bailor	102	capital expenditure	204-205
balance sheet	1, 163, 235	cash	75-84, 94-95, 101-105, 107-108, 173-174, 197
balancing accounts	62-66, 124, 159, 216-217	cash book	47, 75-85,134-136, 175, 197, 211-218

INDEX

CHAPS	90	day book	2, 7, 48, 116-117
cheque	92-93,102-105,132-133, 174	debit card	75, 90-91
cheque guarantee card	93-94	debtor (see sales ledger)	102
cheque requisition	132-133	delivery note	14, 114
contra	79, 143-144	direct credit	90
contract	13, 38-42	direct debit	90, 133
control account	53, 55, 120, 175-178	discount	17-23, 80-83, 87-88, 136, 139
credit card	75, 90-81, 133	double entry	47, 50-56, 118-121, 136-141, 175-179
credit note	24-26	drawings	198, 201, 225
creditor (see purchases ledger)	102	EDI	116
crossing	93	email	188-190

INDEX

errors 222, 226-227, 230-234

expenses 118, 133-134, 155-163, 198, 229, 235

fax 187

financial accounts 4

financial statements 2, 6, 235-236, 246

fixed assets 201, 205, 229, 235-237

float 94-95, 107

floor limit 92

goods received note 114-115

HMRC 2, 15, 34, 52, 170-171, 175, 177, 202-203, 229, 236

imprest method 158

income 235

income tax 170

integrated ledger 47

international terminology 235

inventory (see stock)

invoice 15-22, 27, 48, 115, 124, 131

journal 143, 223-227, 231-233

letter 190-192

limited company 3, 4

loan 102, 199, 229, 236

main ledger 47-48, 51, 55, 56, 60-62, 65-66, 115-117, 119, 155,

INDEX

management accounts 4

memorandum 181-182

mortgagee 102

mortgagor 102

national insurance 170-171, 176-178

non current asset (see fixed asset)

note 184-185

organisational structures 4-6

overdraft 102

partnership 3, 4

payables (see purchase ledger)

PAYE 171

paying-in slip 104-105

payslip 172-173

petty cash 155-163, 197

petty cash voucher 156-158

postal order 88

prepayment card 91-92

prime document 1, 223

principal 102

profit and loss statement 1, 163, 200, 235, 246

purchase order 12-13, 42, 43, 114, 116, 131

INDEX

purchases day book 116-118, 136

purchases ledger 47, 117-119, 121-122, 141-142, 196-197

purchases ledger control account 120-121, 123-124, 139, 141-143, 196

purchases returns day book 121

quote 11-12

receivables (see sales ledger)

reconciliation, 57, 141-142, 218

remittance advice 88-89

returns note 23, 115

revenue expenditure 204-205

Sale of Goods Act 1979 40-41

sales day book 48-50, 52, 54, 57, 58, 231

sales ledger 47, 49, 54, 56, 59-60, 64-65, 84, 97-98, 143-144, 195-196

sales ledger control account 56-57, 61-62, 67, 78-79, 87, 144, 196, 229

sales returns day book 58-59

sole trader 2-3, 4, 7, 42, 224

statement of account 27-28, 86, 115, 132

statement of financial position (see balance sheet)

stock 198, 200, 225, 235

stock 198, 200, 225, 235

suspense account 231-233

'T' account 50,76

INDEX

Trades Description Act 1968 40, 41-42

trial balance 227-230, 233-234

Unfair Contract Terms Act 40, 42

VAT 15, 18, 24-25, 33-37, 157, 202-204

wages 169-179